IMAGES
of America

HOLLAND

THE TULIP TOWN

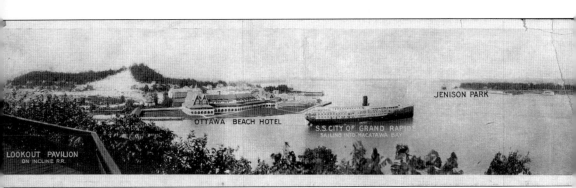

This is a panoramic view of Holland, Michigan life on the lake, photographed in 1913.

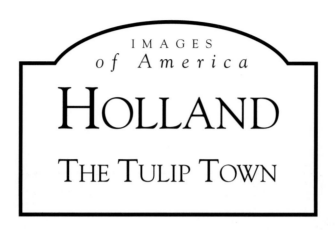

IMAGES
of America

HOLLAND
THE TULIP TOWN

Randall P. Vande Water

ARCADIA

Published by Arcadia Publishing,
an imprint of Tempus Publishing, Inc.
3047 N. Lincoln Ave., Suite 410
Chicago, IL 60657

Printed in Great Britain.

Library of Congress Catalog Card Number: 2002108723

For all general information contact Arcadia Publishing at:
Telephone 843-853-2070
Fax 843-853-0044
E-Mail sales@arcadiapublishing.com

For customer service and orders:
Toll-Free 1-888-313-2665

Visit us on the internet at http://www.arcadiapublishing.com

This book is dedicated to the four generations of people in my life. I would like to dedicate this publication to my late parents, William H. and Kitty A. Vande Water; my wife, Mary Elizabeth; our children, Nancy Ann Vande Water Sivertson, Kathryn Lynn Speeter, and Kenneth Mark Stam; and our grandchildren, E. Jonathan Paul Sivertson, Kristina Hope Sivertson, Sarah Kathryn Sivertson, Marissa Elizabeth Padding, Alexandra Kendall Stam and Nicole Elizabeth Stam.

CONTENTS

ACKNOWLEDGMENTS

Compiling an *Images of America* book on Holland, Michigan was accomplished through the combined efforts of family, friends, and professional organizations. Thanks to these combined efforts, the author is grateful to reveal the community's history, the special categories of its participation in the military, more than a century of resort life, as well as a festival called Tulip Time that will mark its 75th anniversary in 2004. Thousands of pictures have told Holland's story. To glean less than 240 requires a selection process. Some of the chosen photos recall historical moments and specific subjects; other pictures were unique to this community and were chosen strictly for their charm. Special thanks to my wife, Mary Elizabeth, for her interest, help, and encouragement. My late parents, William H. and Kitty Vande Water, saved a variety of pictures. In addition to family snapshots, photographs that illustrated articles written by my father during a 60-year career as a newspaper correspondent were preserved.

Appreciation also goes to *The Holland Sentinel* where some pictures first appeared. A few originated from the Holland Historical Trust of the Joint Archives of Holland collection, while individuals were also kind enough to share their treasures. They include: Robert Beam, Mary Dyke, Paul Essenburg, Douglas Gilbert, Norman Japinga, Yvonne Jonker, Cindy Kuipers, Lawrence McCormick, Marie Nienhuis, Ernest Penna, Carl Poest, Roger Prince, Tino Reyes, Arthur Sas, George Skadding, Mary Vande Wege, Janice Van Lente, Jerry Van Lente, Donald van Reken, Henrietta Veltman, Frances Woltman and Kenneth Zuverink. Some caption information was obtained at Herrick District Library in Holland.

About the Author

Randall P. Vande Water has previously published seven books on Holland history. They include: *On the Way to Today*, (1992), *Holland Happenings, Heroes & Hot Shots, Volumes One, Two, Three, and Four*, (1994, 1995, 1996, 1997) and *Millennium Memories* (1999). *Heinz Holland: A Century of History* was published in 2001. Vande Water co-authored: *The Holland Furnace Company, 1906–1966* (1993) and *And Our Band Plays On: 75 years of the Holland American Legion Band* (1995) with Donald van Reken. Vande Water, a Hope College graduate, spent 40 years as an editor at *The Holland Sentinel*.

INTRODUCTION

These images of Holland, Michigan's life of more than 150 years provide the reader with an opportunity to observe the community's growth and poignantly reflect on an important part of the Midwest.

Beginning on a wind-swept forested swamp in 1847, Holland has advanced to become a vibrant urban center, recognized for its diversity in culture and commerce.

Founded February 9, 1847 by Dr. Albertus Christiaan Van Raalte, the Holland area became home to 1,700 inhabitants in its first year. Incorporated in 1867 with 2,000 residents, the city enjoyed steady growth, and a population of 3,000 welcomed the 20th Century.

Just prior to World War II, the city's population totaled 15,000 people. Steady growth continued during the post-war years, and the community entered the 21st Century with 35,000 people. Including the surrounding townships, Holland boasts 115,000 residents today.

When Van Raalte arrived with his wife, six children, and 53 followers, his group cleared the forest and built log cabins and a church. This group of Dutch men, women, and children tarried on the shores of Lake Macatawa (then Black Lake) after fleeing the potato blight, which caused nationwide agricultural depression, and religious persecution in the Netherlands.

Originally inhabited by Native Americans, who left Ottawa and Allegan counties for northern Michigan in 1849, the Dutch developed the land for farming and other vocations. After the establishment of a public school in 1848, Van Raalte founded a pioneer academy in 1851. Fifteen years later, the academy became Hope College. Included was a seminary with the support of Van Raalte's religious affiliation, the Reformed Church in America. The Western Theological Seminary began in 1883.

On October 9, 1871, the community was devastated when a two-hour early morning fire wiped out more than two-thirds of the city. More than 300 families were left destitute after 212 dwellings and 45 industries were destroyed.

Speaking near the smoldering ruins, Van Raalte said: "Let us remember, God lives. With our Dutch tenacity and our American experience, Holland will be rebuilt." From those ashes came a rebirth, and the founder said at the city's 25th anniversary in 1872: "Because God has built, we live in a happy conviction that He has done well with us and granted our heart's desires... May this inheritance be to you in all eternity, the beloved spot in which you yourselves have learned God, where you have found your God."

In 1882, a church schism split the main Protestant (RCA) denomination in Holland, resulting in the formation of the Christian Reformed Church in America. The first discord within the church had been heard in 1857. The RCA and CRC denominations remain prominent and are the largest in the community today.

Proud of its heritage, Holland built a solid foundation on religion and education, a combination that unlocked doors to the world and gave the increasing populace a particular pride. Holland's 153 churches represent 42 denominations.

In addition to the college and seminary, Holland is home to the Meijer campus of Grand Valley State University and the Holland campus of Davenport University.

One example of Holland's heritage is its impressive Tulip Time festival, which began in 1929. Celebrating the community's Dutch heritage each May, the festival annually attracts more than half a million visitors. There are six million tulips in hundreds of varieties, costumed children and adults scrubbing streets, television and motion picture entertainers, plus parades with more than 50 bands. The 2002 festival included a Mexican fiesta motif, enhancing a Latino festival started here in 1965.

In 1965, a 125-foot windmill, imported from the Netherlands, was opened as a tourist attraction by Prince Bernhard of the Netherlands.

The last half-century has brought about a change in Holland's complexion and the loss of its provincialism. After World War II, Hispanics followed migrant workers from southwestern states, as well as Mexico, to work in Holland industries. Annexation in the late 1950s increased the city's size and placed Holland in two counties. Two-thirds of Holland, the original city, is located in Ottawa County, while one-third is in Allegan County.

In the 1960s, Hispanics arrived from Cuba and other locations, followed in the 1970s by Southeast Asians, and during the last decade African-Americans have settled here. Ethnic minorities constitute one quarter of Holland's city population. Twenty-two percent is Hispanic.

Holland is located 150 miles north of Chicago, 175 miles west of Detroit, and 25 miles west of Grand Rapids. It started attracting visitors in the last quarter of the 19th Century. Visitors chose the sugar sand of Lake Michigan and the tree-filled sand dunes as ideal places to vacation. Resort hotels, constructed as the 19th century concluded, brought people by ship and train to enjoy the summer breezes provided by the small lake and its channel that flows into Lake Michigan.

Resorting and tourism continue to be major attractions in Holland. The 75-year-old state park at Ottawa Beach leads the state in attendance, drawing more than 1.7 million visitors each year. With a strong industrial base of manufacturing and production of furniture, food, boats, mirrors, and automobile supplies, the Holland area has seen unprecedented growth. With the help of local airports, and the Gerald R. Ford International Airport which lies less than an hour away, Holland has become a destination for all ages.

Pictures in this publication capture Holland's flavor. They provide a glimpse at the century of Dutch tradition when the telephone directory contained mostly Dutch names. Directories now illustrate the cultural and commercial tastes and fashions of the times.

Holland's history of military participation, which includes four Medal of Honor recipients, highlights human interest vignettes. The photos emphasize elements of life known, past and present, in our hometown of Holland, nestled near the shores of Lake Michigan.

One

ON THE WAY
FROM YESTERDAY

(1847–1900)

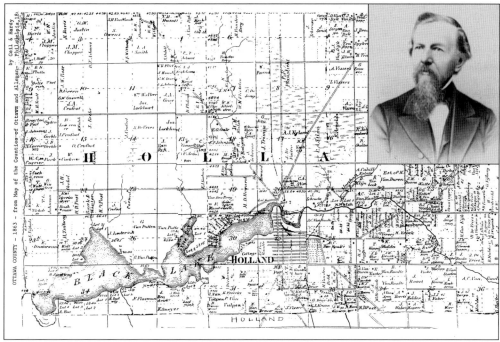

Holland, Michigan was incorporated on March 25, 1867. This map of Holland and a portion of Ottawa County to the north was drawn in 1863 by the Philadelphia, Pennsylvania firm of Geil & Hardy. The south border of Holland was Sixteenth Street. Black Lake was connected to Lake Michigan (not shown) by a channel at the far left.

Dr. Albertus Christiaan Van Raalte (October 17, 1811–November 7, 1876) founded the settlement of Holland in 1847.

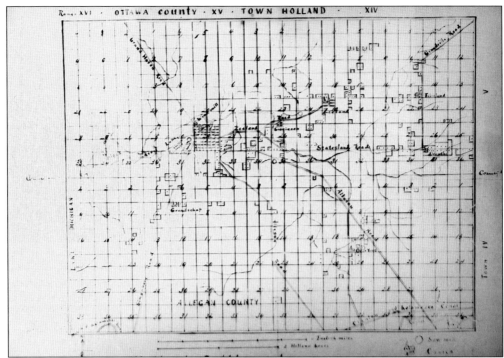

This is the Holland, Michigan settlement in 1849. It was founded by Dr. A.C. Van Raalte and six other people, including one woman, on February 9, 1847. Van Raalte's family and a group of 53 left the Netherlands on September 24, 1846 on the *Southerner*, arriving in New York on November 17, 1846. The other settlements noted began later in 1847.

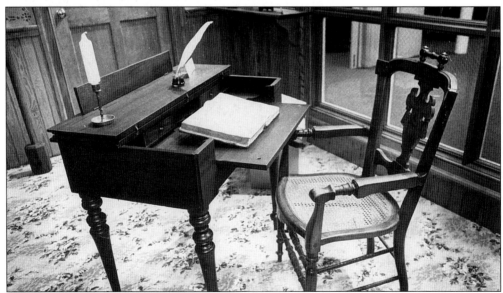

This is the table and chair where Dr. A.C. Van Raalte sat and wrote his weekly sermons. In addition, he conducted much of the church, school, and township business. The furniture is now on display at the Pillar Christian Reformed Church in Holland. This building was dedicated June 25, 1856.

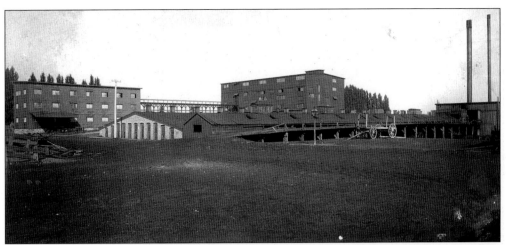

The Cappon-Bertsch Leather Company was located on West Eighth Street, present site of the Civic Center. Following the devastating fire of October 9, 1871, which destroyed the original factory and much of the town, this building was constructed in 1872. The property was owned by Isaac Cappon, Holland's first mayor, and John Bertsch of Grand Rapids, Michigan. Founded in 1857, the business consisted of tanning hides and skins. The firm was aided by Civil War government contracts for leather. By 1894, the company had capital stock of $400,000; it handled 100,000 hides and 30,000 skins annually for sole, harness, and saddle leather. The company had 400 employees and four traveling salesmen nationwide.

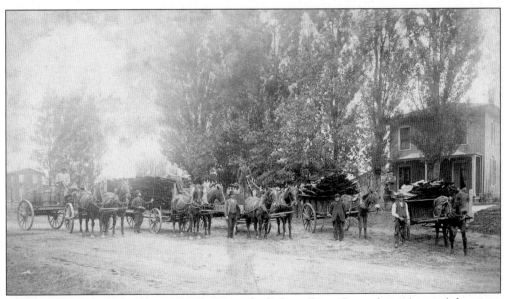

Teams of horses brought Eastern Hemlock tree bark down River Street (now Avenue) for use at the Cappon-Bertsch Leather Company on Pine Avenue and Eighth Street in the 1870s. With the hemlock's "tannin-rich" bark, this tree became a vital resource for tanning leather. One such Eastern Hemlock tree is located on the Van Raalte Farm on East Sixteenth Street. The plaque next to the tree indicates that the Cappon-Bertsch Leather Company used "mountains of Hemlock bark to produce shoe leather from 1858 until the 1930s." The plaque notes the tree has flourished in the "deep, cool, perpetually moist earth for over 200 years and may live over 600 years." Common to the Great Lakes, the hemlocks were here before the Holland settlement.

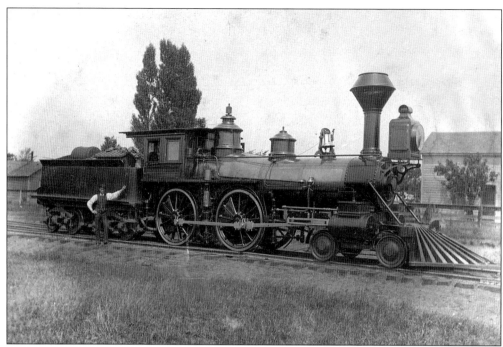

Railroads began in Holland in 1870. One of the first trains was a Chicago and West Michigan locomotive in the early 1870s. The front of the train had a steel wedge-shaped "cow-catcher" frame attached for clearing tracks.

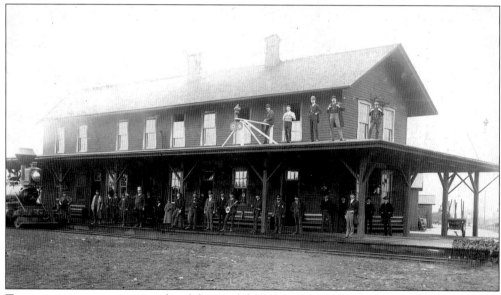

Twenty passenger trains arrived and departed daily in 1895 at the Chicago and West Michigan Railroad Depot. Telegraph operators stood under the canopy. Holland's second depot, this facility faced east. It was in the center of the Allegan, Michigan Y track. Trains from the Michigan cities of Grand Haven and Muskegon came from the west and crossed over a curved trestle passing Black River near Central Avenue at Fourth Street. After loading, trains would "Y" onto the Allegan division.

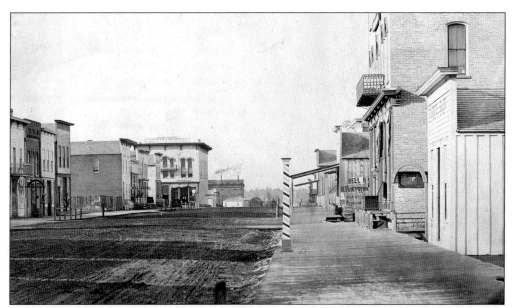

Early on October 9, 1877, six years after fire had destroyed two-thirds of Holland, fire again ravaged downtown Holland. Surviving the blaze in the right foreground were the City Hotel and its balcony. Pictured in this post-fire scene is the former Kenyon Opera House (center), which was rebuilt by attorney Patrick McBride and Hope College professor Dowe Yntema. Appearing at the left front are the following: Lumblatt's Saloon, Van Duren's Shoes, a fence protecting Mrs. Koningsburg's flowers, followed by her husband's, Charles Koningburg, Germania House (hotel), Kuite's Meat Market, Pete Brown's Saloon, and Engbertus Vander Veen's Hardware. The Hummel Tannery smokestacks on the southeast corner of Eighth Street and Pine Avenue are in the background.

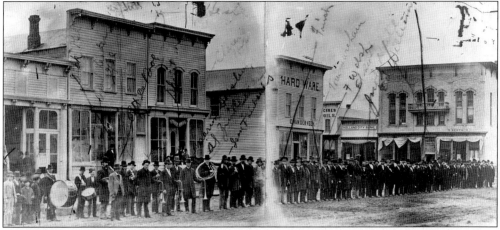

These Holland men, some identified, along with a local band, assembled on Eighth Street for the weekly Market Day. It was held for the first time in 1882. Market Days were held for several months each year. Nearby farmers would bring produce to sell in the city. The *Holland City News* said: "Drunken brawls were frequent in those days between the 'town blood' and the 'country boys' and [there was] only one marshal to handle the wayward." The building at right with the balcony, on River Street (Avenue), was similar to the wooden opera house that had burned in 1877. Vander Veen's Hardware is across the street.

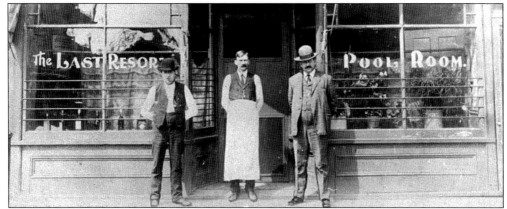

In the 1890s, Holland's Last Resort was a popular saloon and pool room. Located on East Eighth Street near the train depot, the Last Resort signified the last chance for a person to get a drink before boarding a train. It was also the first place in Holland for disembarking passengers to buy a drink.

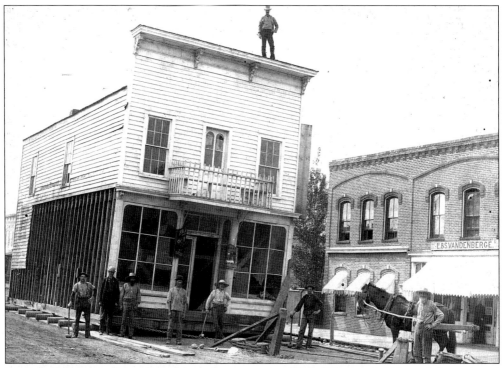

Sutton's Saloon was located on the southeast corner of Eighth Street and Central Avenue and was owned by E.F. Sutton, the city's beer baron, in 1874. The saloon was a part of his brewery business. Arend D. Bosman purchased the building in the mid-1880s for a "second hand" store and moved the building a block east. Eighth Street was comprised of a clay and gravel road, and the two-story building was moved on heavy rollers placed under the edifice at the rear and then carried to the front again. Moving the rig were Civil War veteran William H. Finch (who fired the Centennial Park cannon every July 4,) Art Drinkwater, Frank Stansbury, Hank Lindemeyer, Jake Dogger, Bill Van Anroy, and Adsel Gale, who owned the horse which turned the apparatus that moved the house.

This church, initially called the First Reformed Church, was dedicated June 25, 1856. Dr. A.C. Van Raalte served the six-pillar church that survived the fire of 1871. Van Raalte resigned from his pastorate in 1867. Torn by dissension in 1879, the congregation seceded from the Reformed Church in America in 1882. Separatists had established the Christian Reformed Church in 1857. Seceders joined in 1884 and remained in the building. Formerly named Ninth Street CRC, the church is located at 57 East Tenth Street and called Pillar CRC.

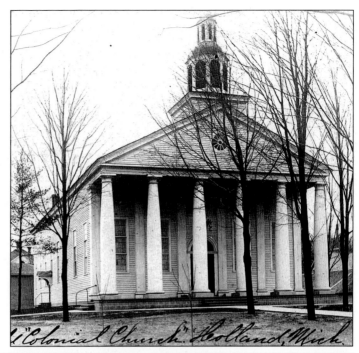

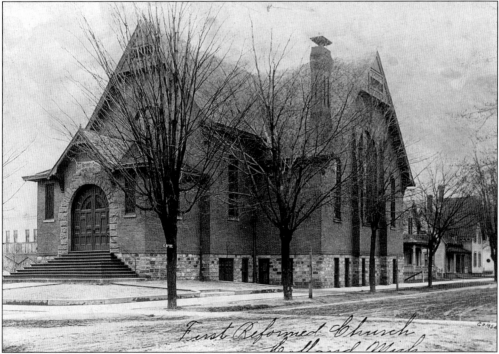

This church was built in 1884 by a group of Reformed Church in America members who had earlier attended Pillar Church. The building was constructed by members of the regrouped First RCA and located at 4 East Ninth Street, a block west of the Pillar Church. A new building opened in January 1963 at 630 State Street. The Salvation Army occupied the old building before it was demolished in the 1990s.

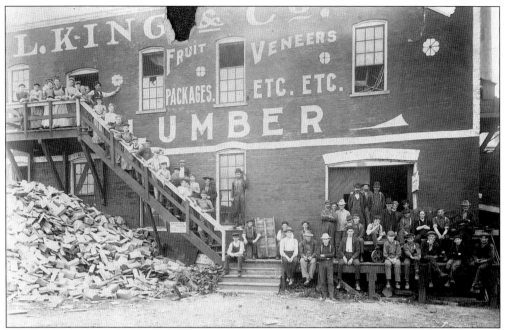

Organized in 1892 and moving to Holland eight years later, the C.L. King Basket Factory was located on Black Lake (Lake Macatawa) and was the largest firm of its kind in Michigan. Utilizing the Chicago and West Michigan railroad, as well as the proximity of lumber, the company made peach and grape baskets, butter-dish plates, fruit packages, wood plates, veneers, and berry boxes. The 150-by-350-foot building included a power house and dry kilns. King, who had moved the company from Montague, Michigan, was resident partner and superintendent. By 1900, he manufactured 120,000 baskets, 75,000,000 butter plates, and 2,000,000 fruit packages annually. Located on the present site of Kollen Park, the factory was torn down in 1917.

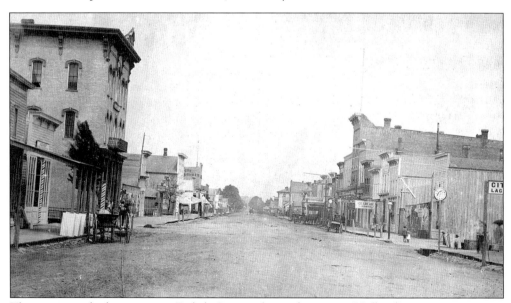

This is a view looking east on Eighth Street, always downtown Holland's main street, more than 125 years ago. The City Hotel is at left.

16

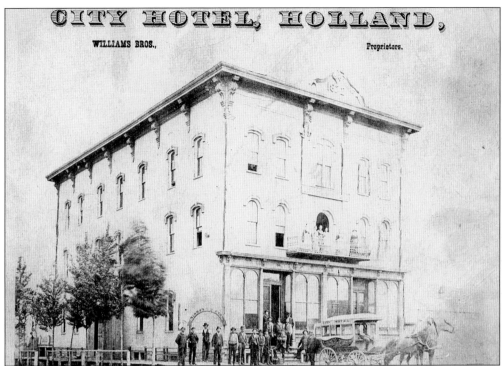

Constructed by William Kellogg in 1872, the City Hotel stood three stories tall and had a balcony on the second floor where the female employees are standing. It had a capacity of 50 guests. In front is the hotel's "bus" driven by Holland's first African-American resident, named Silas, who came to the city June 7, 1873. Frequently remodeled and the winner of excellence awards, the facility was named Hotel Holland in 1898 and remained on the site until March 10, 1924, when it was demolished to make room for the Warm Friend Tavern.

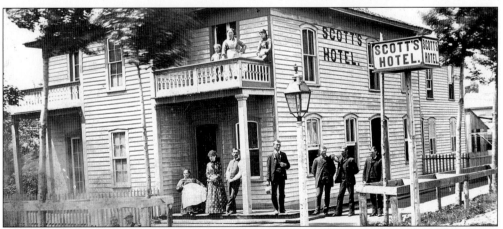

Scott's Hotel opened in 1877 on the northwest corner of Ninth Street and Columbia Avenue. Located a block west of the train depot, the hotel was frequented by train passengers. Built by William J. Scott and his wife, Blanche, the Scotts arrived in Holland before the 1871 fire. They came from New York where they had lived along the Erie Canal. Scott died on November 20, 1904 and his wife died on August 29, 1913. The hotel was turned into a rooming house for Hope College students in the early 1900s, and was demolished for a parking lot in March 1989.

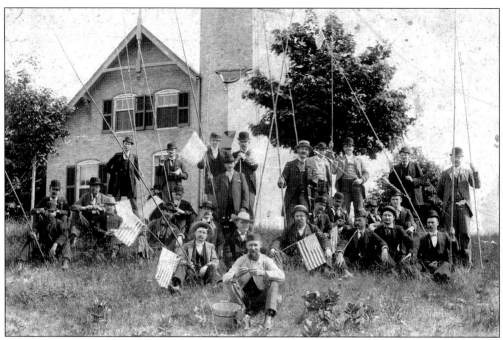

These patriotic Holland fishermen were photographed in 1889 when the United States flag contained 42 stars.

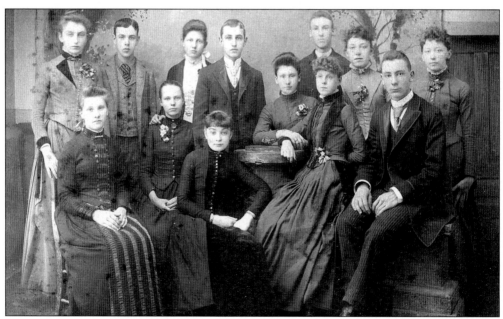

Three men were members of the 1890 Holland High School graduating class. Graduates were Marie S. Damson, Jennie De Vries, Nellie D. Huntley, Beatrice L. Kimpton, John Elenbaas, Gerrit Steketee, Anthony Van Ry, Lou E. Markham, Nella Pfanstiehl, Henrietta Van den Berg, and Alice M. Purdy. J.W. Humphrey was superintendent and Miss Delia Cook was principal. Five women composed Holland High School's first graduating class in 1873. By 1890, 10 of the 57 graduates were men.

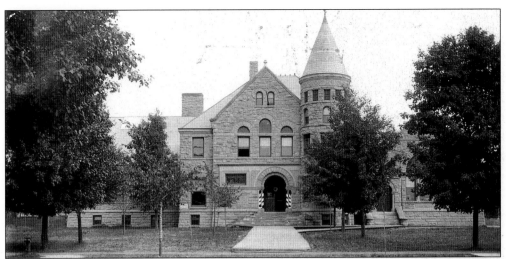

Graves Hall and Winants Chapel were dedicated on the Hope College campus June 26, 1894. Nathan F. Graves, president of the New York Banking Company of Syracuse, New York, donated $10,700 for the library to bear his name and to purchase works needed by different departments. Mrs. Gerrit Winants of Bergen Point, New Jersey donated $10,000 in memory of her husband, who was a New York shipbuilder. Graves and the Winants were members of the Reformed Church in America. Hope is affiliated with the RCA. Constructed of Waverly stone, quarried a mile east of Holland, the buildings contain classrooms and an auditorium.

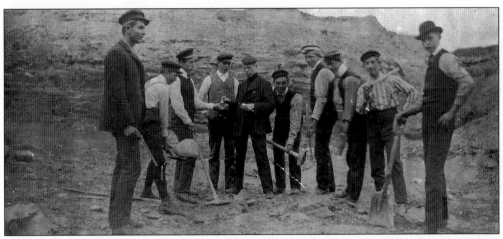

Waverly Stone Company workers pause in the quarry in the early 1900s. Waverly stone, a fine-grained, bluish-gray siliceous sandstone, was discovered in the banks of the Black River in 1848. Since the stone had first been developed in Waverly, Ohio, the type found in Holland was given the same name. The first practical use for the stone was discovered in 1857, when a quantity was quarried and moved by scows to Holland. It was used in the construction of the foundation and basement walls of the dormitory Van Vleck Hall, when Hope College was a Pioneer Academy. (Hope opened in 1866.) Flourishing for years, the Waverly Stone Company constructed many buildings in Western Michigan. Its busiest time was during the last decade of the 19th Century. By the early 1920s, the company discontinued because cement blocks were more popular for construction. The quarry where the stone was harvested is located east of M-21, a few hundred yards northeast of 120th Avenue and Waverly Road. The Van Duren family purchased the property in 1927 and built a home adjacent to the placid, clear quarry.

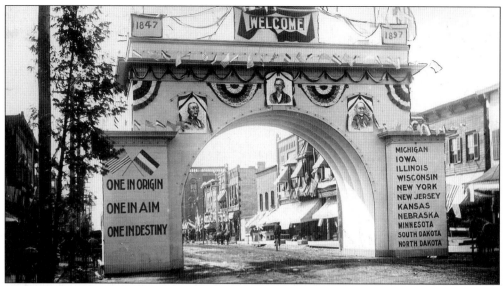

Highlighting Holland's celebration of its 50th Anniversary on August 25 and 26, 1897, a wooden arch covered with canvas was constructed over Eighth Street. The structure was 32 feet high and 47 feet wide and was placed near the "principal thoroughfare (Eighth Street) near Central Avenue." "Illumined by 200 incandescents and decorated with flags and bunting, the arch spanned the street from curb to curb," *The Holland Daily Sentinel* said. Pictures of town founders, Dr. Van Raalte of Holland, Rev. Cornelius Vander Meulen of Zeeland, Michigan, and Rev. Hendrik P. Scholte of Pella, Iowa, were placed on the arch near the names of the 11 states where immigrants from the Netherlands had settled in the United States. The Rottschafer Brothers of Holland built the arch.

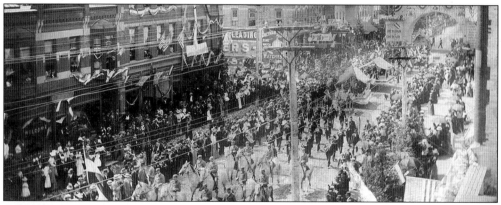

Holland's "Semi-Centennial Celebration of the Holland Immigration and Colonization in the United States" in 1897 attracted an estimated crowd of 20,000 to 30,000 visitors. A parade started at 10:30 a.m. and took 35 minutes to pass. Featured were mounted police, U.S and Dutch flags, 25 Native Americans, 19 floats, Phinney's band, 1847 settlers in carriages, four generations of the De Feyter family, 1847 log cabin, immigrant baggage wagon, flower girls, 43 women representing the various states, Civil War veterans, and Mary Vander Haar depicting the Queen of the Netherlands. Other units included a woman wearing a 1551 bridal "costume," a woman representing the Goddess of Liberty, delegations from Grand Rapids, Muskegon, Zeeland, city drum corps, city officials and the fire department. Speeches, a 315-voice chorus, a band concert, and fireworks concluded the celebration in Centennial Park.

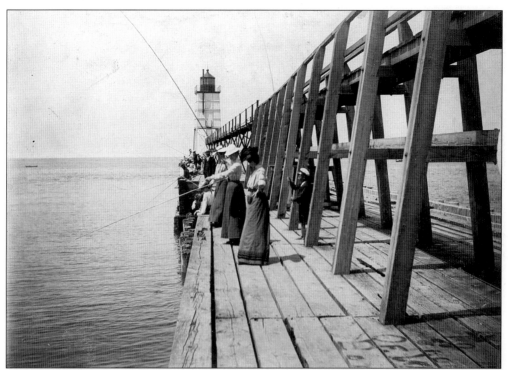

The wooden pier which reached out into Lake Michigan provided an excellent place for women and men to fish for yellow perch. In the background is the lighthouse. The first lighthouse was a small wooden structure built in 1872. In 1880, the lighthouse service installed a new light in a protective cage atop a metal pole. A steel tower was constructed in 1900.

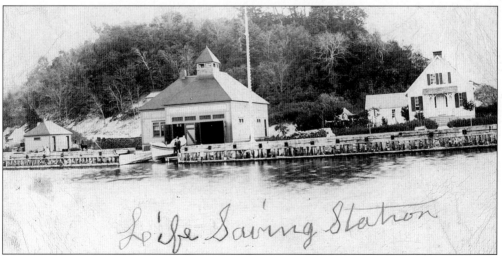

After approval for a life-saving station was granted in August 1883, the station opened for service and a new patrol boat arrived in August 1886. Capt. Charles Morton was in charge of the station. He was paid $700. The crew included: August Morrison, Adam Weckler, Andrew Miller, William Robinson, William Baker, Charles Paget, and John Smith. They were paid $400 each and their duties lasted 24 hours during the season, which began in March. The crew worked two-hour day watches and four-hour night watches.

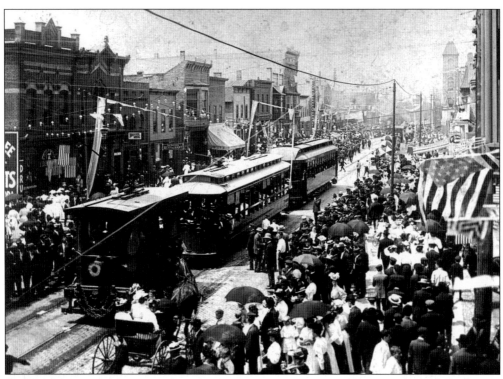

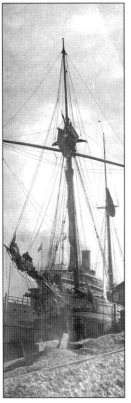

On July 4, 1898, the first Interurban electric railroad car to carry passengers arrived in Holland. The first rails in Holland had been laid by the Holland and Lake Michigan Railway at River (Avenue) and Eighth Street. These cars are on the track a half-block east of there. More than 100 men and 17 teams of horses constructed the line. The payroll for construction workers was $1,000 weekly. The trains ran from Grand Rapids through Grandville, Jenison, Shack Huddle, Jamestown, Forest Grove, Vriesland, Zeeland, Holland, Jenison Park, Macatawa Park, and Saugatuck. The Interurban freight office was on Eighth Street near Pine Avenue. The passenger train continued south on River and turned west on 13th Street. The line continued near South Shore Drive, stopping near Sunnybrook Station at Virginia Park. Extending south near 160th Street, the train headed to Castle Park and Saugatuck. The train met its demise November 15, 1926.

The first time a passenger ship connected Holland directly with Chicago, via Lake Michigan, was July 4, 1889, when the *Mabel Bradshaw* docked at the foot of Fifth Street at the old Harrington Dock. That first year the ship made four trips a week, leaving Holland on Sunday, Monday, Wednesday, and Friday evenings, after the arrival of trains at 6:35 p.m. The fare was $2 one way or $3.50 round trip. Owner Hugh Bradshaw named the ship after his daughter Mabel. She was to christen the ship with a bottle of champagne. As she reached for the bow, the bottle slipped from her hand and fell into the water, leaving the ship unchristened. The ship was used for a ferrying service a few years later and spent its last years on Lake Superior.

Two
THE OLD HOMETOWN
(1900–1920)

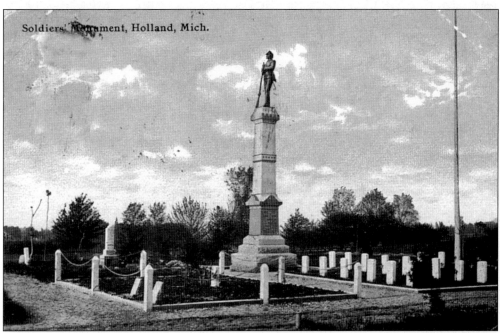

Soldiers' Monument, Holland, Mich.

The Soldier's Monument in Pilgrim Home Cemetery in Holland was dedicated May 30, 1902. Spearheaded by the A.C. Van Raalte Post of the Grand Army of the Republic, the Holland Civil War veterans collected $1,117 for the monument in a fund drive that started in 1894. The monument's base is inscribed with the names of 31 Holland men who never returned. It reads: "Our absent dead—volunteered from Holland in defense of the Union and never returned. They lie buried in known and unknown graves in the South."

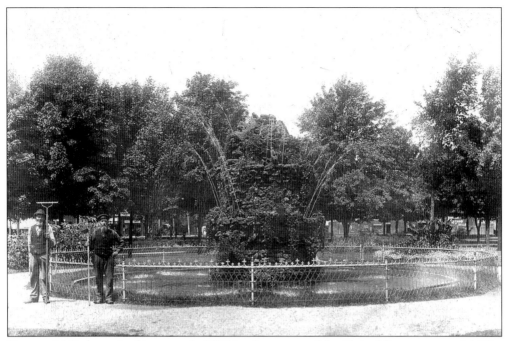

Centennial Park received its name in 1876 in observance of the United States centennial. The four-block section is bordered on the east and west by Central and River Avenues and on the north and south by Tenth and Twelfth Streets. Trees were first planted in the park in 1876 and the fountain and pond were placed in the center, at the spot formerly occupied by a flag pole. The fountain was dedicated in 1902. Johannes (John) Van Lente (right) was gardener for the city of Holland and helped design the stone fountain. He is pictured here, standing with his fellow gardener Henry John Slighter. Both men had served in the Civil War.

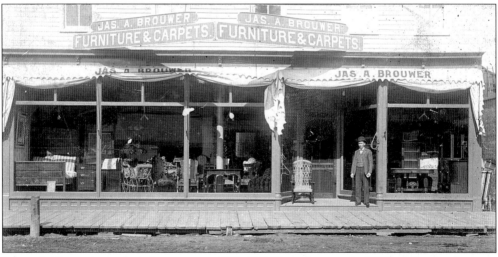

James A. Brouwer purchased property at 212–216 River Avenue in 1899 and erected a store with a 40-foot storefront. Selling furniture and carpets, Brouwer began his merchant career at age 18 in 1872 and started selling furniture on the second floor of an Eighth Street building. For many years he drove a 1925 Detroit Edison electric car to and from the furniture store. Brouwer died in 1950 at age 96.

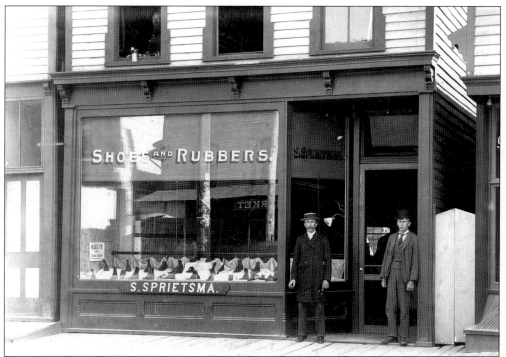

In 1915, Simon Sprietsma, and his son, Nicholas, operated a shoe store at 28 West Eighth Street. Lucas Sprietsma, the store's founder, had his first store at 18 West Eighth Street, and in 1894 it moved to its location at East Eighth Street. Nicholas later served as Holland City Treasurer, and in 1936, he was elected and served one two-year term as Ottawa County Treasurer. He was the last Democrat to hold office in Ottawa County.

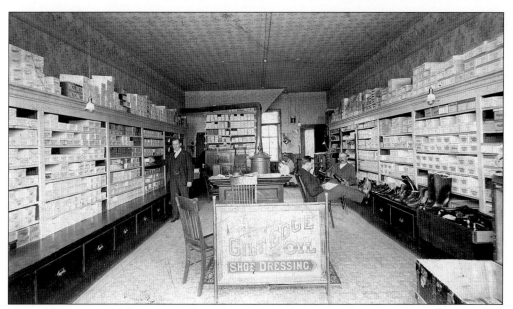

This is the interior of Sprietsma's Shoe Store where they were advertising "The Giltedge Oil" shoe dressing.

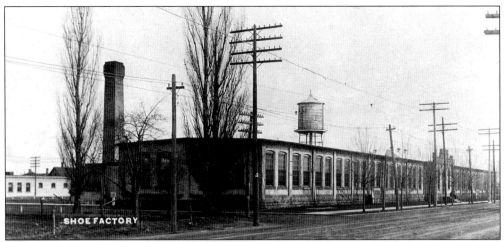

The Holland Shoe Company was established in 1895. The company came from Racine, Wisconsin. The firm was attracted by a property incentive called the Bonus Plan. In 1939, the Holland plant merged with a shoe company in Racine, which moved all of its operations here. It then became the Holland-Racine Shoe Company. The company closed in 1967 and H.J. Heinz purchased the office building.

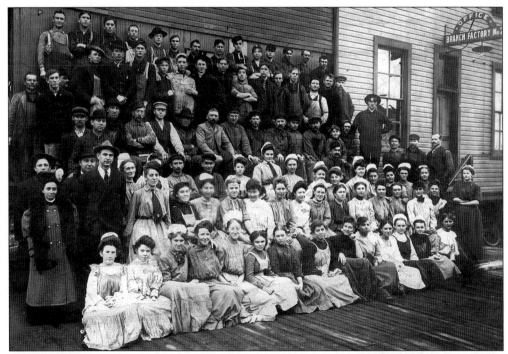

On January 20, 1897, the H.J. Heinz Company announced plans to erect a facility in Holland. In 1906, favorable business conditions saw the plant grow from one small building to eight edifices. These employees were photographed in front of the office of the Heinz Branch Factory No. 7. The wooden building was the first constructed and was called the cooper shop. The office was a part of it. Heinz marked its 100th anniversary in Holland in 1997, and is the only industry in Holland's history to span three centuries under the same ownership and product line. Heinz in Holland is the largest pickle factory in the world.

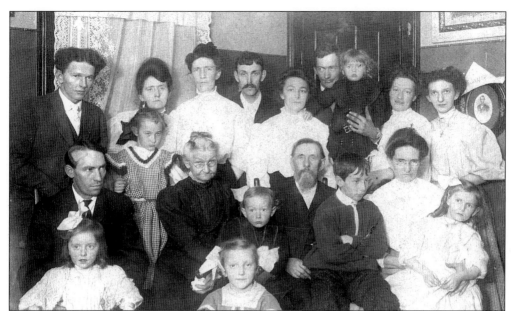

Johannes Van Lente (center, bearded) arrived in Holland, Michigan in the early fall of 1847. A 12-year-old boy from Zwolle, the Netherlands, Van Lente left Amsterdam on the *Albatross*, on June 1, 1847, with his parents, six siblings, and sister-in-law. They arrived in New York on July 12, 1847. Upon his return from the Civil War, he was married to Jantje Bouwman by Dr. A.C. Van Raalte. The couple was photographed in 1907 with their children, spouses, and grandchildren. Abraham Lincoln's portrait is on the wall. Members of the family are, as follows: (bottom row) Adeline Vander Hill, Janet De Graaf; (middle row) James Vander Hill, Geneva Van Lente, Jantje Bouwman Van Lente, Kenneth Van Lente, Johannes Van Lente, Franklyn Van Ry, Anna Van Lente Van Ry, Kitty Van Ry; (top row) Ralph Van Lente, Jennie Van Lente Vander Hill, Mary Van Lente De Graaf, Anthony Van Ry, Johanna De Cook Van Lente, Frederick Van Lente, Earl Van Lente, Gertrude Reidsema Van Lente, and Edith De Graaf Boylan.

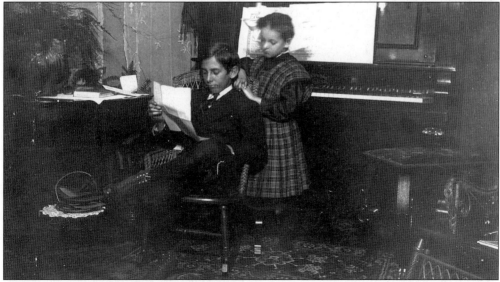

Brother and sister Franklyn and Kitty Van Ry study their music before a piano lesson in 1910.

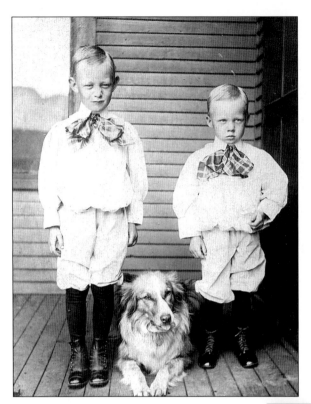

Standing on the porch in 1906 at 187 East 13th Street in Holland, brothers William H. and Bernard Vande Water flank their dog Shep. Dressed in knickers and white shirts, the boys are sporting plaid ties.

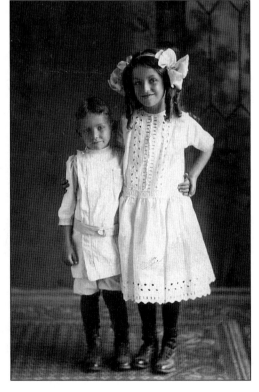

Dressed in their finest and ready to attend church are Martha Knipe and her brother Alenis of 172 Central Avenue. The picture was taken a block away in Hoffman Studio, at 232 River Street, in 1910.

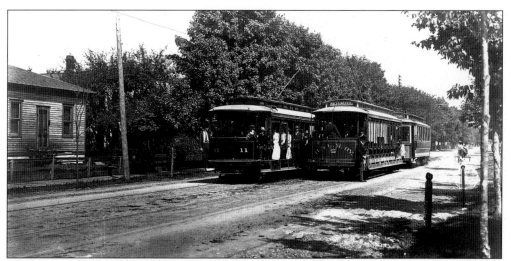

A buggy passes on the far right, while three Interurban trains stop on River Avenue, between Eighth Street and 13th Street, in Holland. The H & LM Railway had two tracks in 1900 and $150,000 in stock. The electric train on the left is heading north while the two other cars are heading south and will turn west to head to the resort area at Macatawa Park. The Interurban enjoyed its era for a quarter century, carrying thousands of passengers and tons of freight. Between 1901 and 1926, the Interurban was involved in 49 fatal accidents.

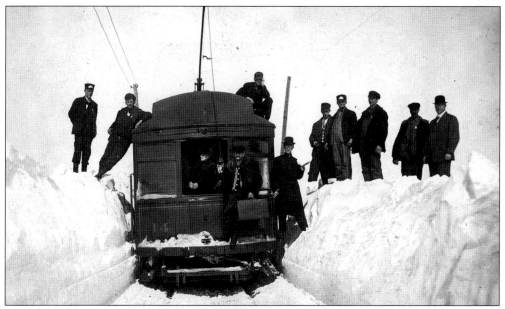

Interurban electric trains operated on tracks through deep snowdrifts. This train is at Sunnybrook Station looking south, near Eugene Teusink's Farm at A-6343 147th Avenue. Trolleys were crowded during winter because passengers wanted to see the snow covered surroundings and Lake Michigan during winter storms. The snow was cleared by hand and V-shaped snow plows, stored at car barns. One of the biggest car barns was at Virginia Park, where fire destroyed the barn, ten passenger cars, and a snow plow on January 10, 1900. The damages totaled $40,000, and $31,000 was covered by insurance. Three replacement cars arrived March 23 from Philadelphia and regular service began October 14, 1901, after a car barn was constructed.

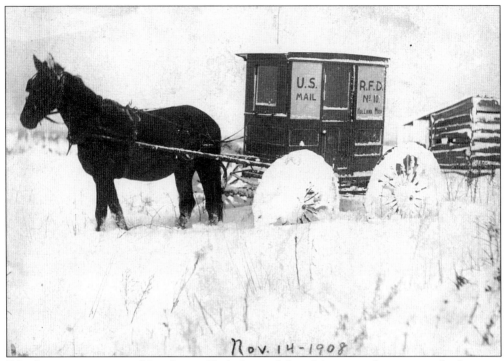

Nov. 14-1908

"Neither rain nor snow..." Lambertus Tinholt, rural free delivery mail carrier used a horse to deliver the mail in the snow on November 14, 1908.

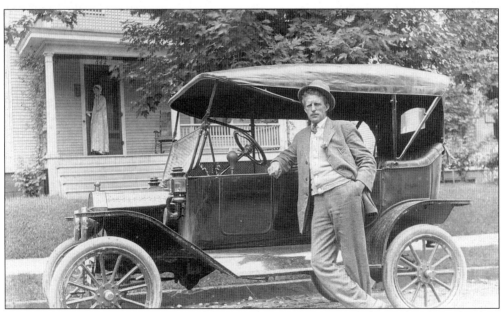

Leonard Kievit leans on his 1912 Model T Ford car while a young lady watches from the door of her home.

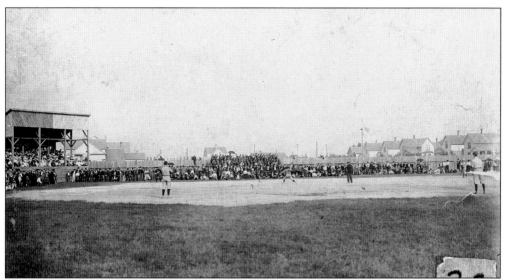

Crowds surrounded the Nineteenth Street and College Avenue field to watch Holland teams play baseball in the early 1900s. Cleveland shortstop Neal Ball of Holland, who completed the first unassisted triple play in the major leagues July 19, 1909, played on this field. In 1910 and 1911, Holland competed in the Class D West Michigan League and the Class D Michigan State League. The Holland team was called the Independents.

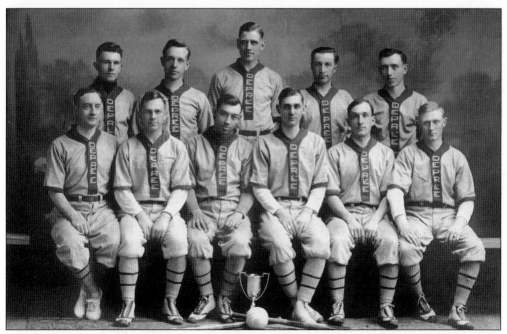

Indoor and outdoor softball thrived in Holland during the first decade of the 20th Century. The indoor games would be played in a school auditorium or gymnasium. This team, displaying its winning trophy, represented the De Pree Chemical Company, of 101 Central Avenue. The firm manufactured pharmaceuticals. Company manager Con De Pree was an outstanding baseball player. He managed the Holland team from 1899 to 1903 and also owned stock in the Holland Baseball Association, which supported the Michigan State League Holland team.

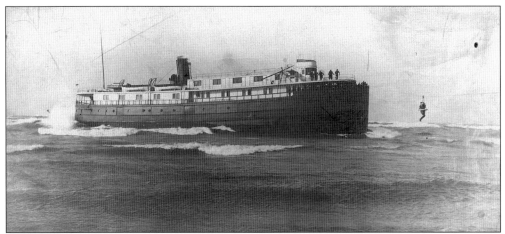

Passengers and crew were rescued by a breeches buoy from the stuck steamer *Argo* on November 24, 1905. Carrying 23 passengers and a crew of 32, the *Argo* encountered a terrific southwest gale on Lake Michigan and struck a sand bar about 1,500 feet from the north pier, 400 feet from shore and north of Holland Harbor. A cannon shot landed the whipline on the ship's deck on the second try. A surfman from the life-saving station scrambled up the side of the ship and assisted the people with the breeches buoy. Mrs. P.J. Niskern of Big Rapids was the first in the buoy. Three other women and a 10-year-old girl were brought to safety. After 15 passengers had been hauled to shore, the line broke. The line was again shot and the remainder of passengers and crew were rescued. The *Argo* stayed beached until January 28, 1906 when it was released with a towline strung from a tug. The ship's hull was not damaged and the ship left for Manitowoc, Wisconsin.

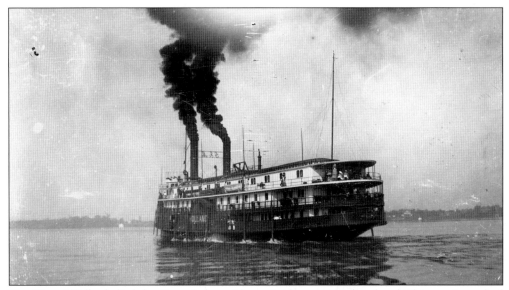

The *City of Holland* plied the Great Lakes with service between Holland and Chicago. Launched April 10, 1893 in Saugatuck with a single smokestack, the ship sailed for 41 years. More than 4,500 people witnessed the launching of the 154-foot ship. Miss Myrtle Beach, daughter of former Holland Mayor W.H. Beach, broke the baptismal bottle over the bow. A second smokestack was added as yearly volume increased and the line was one of the most prosperous and popular lake routes early in the 20th Century. The ship was later purchased by Goodrich Lines and sailed until 1934. The ship "died under the cutter's torch" in 1940 in Sturgeon Bay, Wisconsin.

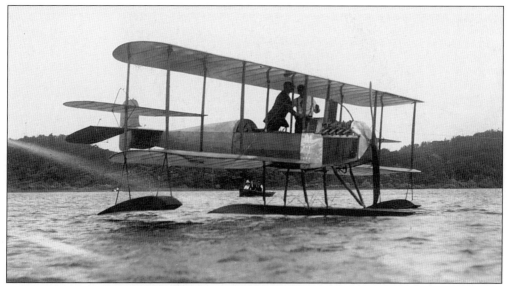

On July 11, 1913 a hydroplane landed on Black (Macatawa) Lake. The *Holland City News* said: "Many people waited hours for the arrival of the flying boat, and a goodly crowd of enthusiastic spectators greeted with cheers, Havens and Ver Planck when they sailed gracefully over old Baldhead, circled the lake like an enormous bird, and finally settled near Lakeside. Havens put on full speed from the landing place to the clubhouse and the speed of the craft in the water as well as in the air is astonishing. Beckwith Havens and J. Ver Planck, owners, arrived in Macatawa with their 100 horsepower Curtis machine at 6:56 p.m., having made the 45 mile trip from South Haven in 56 minutes in the face of strong winds." The plane had first landed on the Kalamazoo River at Saugatuck.

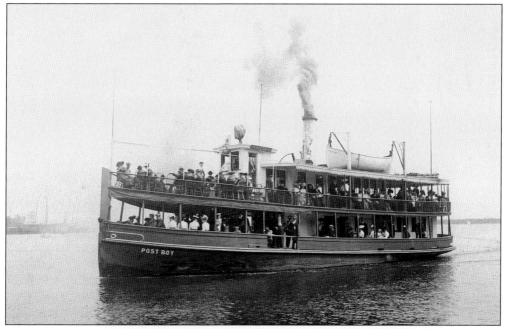

Post Boy was a popular small ferry boat taking people to the resorts, hotels, and beaches at Macatawa Park, Jenison Park, Waukazoo, and Ottawa Beach in the early 1900s.

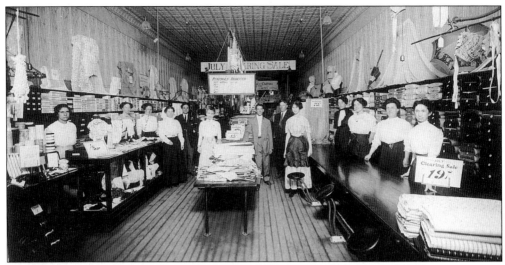

In addition to dry goods, bedding, blankets, and fabrics, this 33 West Eighth Street store was featuring a special price on parasols during a July summer sale. Owned by Bastian Steketee, the store had 10 female sales clerks. The store was 110 feet long and 22 feet wide. Steketee's other Holland store sold groceries at 185 River Avenue.

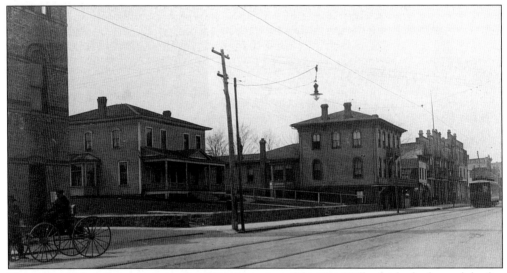

This is East Eighth Street in the early 1900s. A portion of the City Hall, which also housed the fire department, is at left. Rufus Kanters' family home, away from the street, is next to it. Kanters, Holland mayor in 1885 and 1886, introduced a Dutch mode of harbor building by tying together bundles of brush and sinking them down with stones. The branches would swell and prevent the sand from sifting through. Kanters built Holland's first harbor. Born in the Netherlands in 1826, where he developed the brush system, Kanters came to the United States in 1862. His system was also used in Chicago, Illinois; Velasco, Texas; Buffalo, New York; and Coney Island, New York. In 1881, he opened a hardware store on West Eighth Street which two of his sons began operating five years later. In addition to selling building, manufacturing, and tradesmen materials, Kanters Brothers sold home furnishings, stoves, ranges, painters' supplies, and agricultural tools. They were licensed plumbers and their business served as Holland's largest facility of its type in the early 20th Century. Their sister, Jennie, was city librarian for many years.

On June 16, 1904, the Citizens Band (top) was organized in Holland. They presented summer lawn concerts and performed at patriotic events. Damson's Orchestra (bottom) entertained Holland audiences and Macatawa Hotel summer resort guests in 1910.

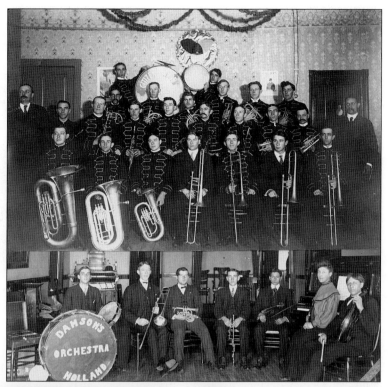

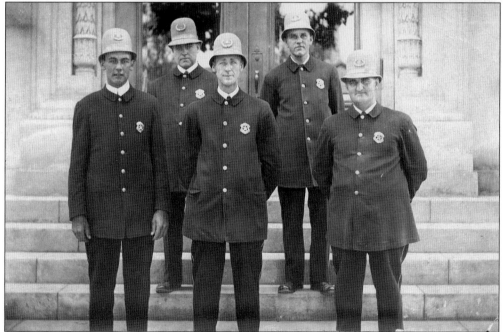

Although they resemble British bobbies from the English police force, these are members of the Holland police force in 1913. The kettle-like helmets were standard equipment. Standing, from left to right, are as follows: Frank Austin, Dave O'Connor, Jack Wagner, Cornelius Steketee, and Simon Meeusen.

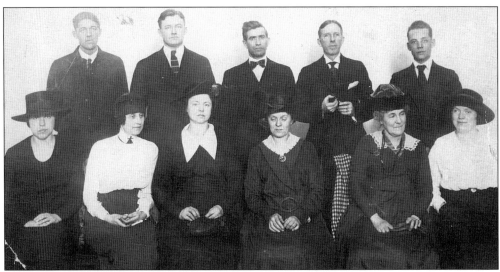

In a slander case, nicknamed a "chicken case," between two local women, Holland's first all-female jury said "guilty" on March 4, 1919. Jury members, seated from left to right, are as follows: Jeannette Mulder, Mrs. William (Margaret) Olive, Mrs. Egbert (Elizabeth) Fell, Mrs. Frederick (Anna) Aldworth, Mrs. William (Helen) Wing and Mrs. Charles (Elizabeth) Drew. Also pictured, standing, are as follows: police officer Peter Bontekoe, Judge Thomas Robinson, Prosecutor Fred T. Miles, and attorneys Daniel Ten Cate and Clarence Lokker, who represented the defendant. The complainant, Mrs. Mamie O'Connor, claimed the defendant, Mrs. Elizabeth Gilmore, had stolen and eaten her cooked chicken. Mrs. Gilmore was found guilty and was assessed a fine and costs of $61.45. The reason a female jury was selected, according to *The Holland Daily Sentinel*, was because suffrage was a major topic and women were soon to vote. An election was held the following day, March 5, and Holland women voted for the first time. Of 1,033 registered voters, 208 women cast ballots. The male vote was "less than one in five." The case was appealed to the Ottawa County Circuit Court where a 12-man jury upheld the decision.

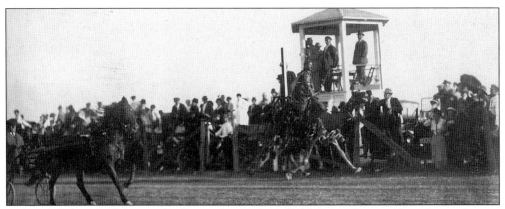

A camel defeated a horse and sulky at the 1916 Holland Fair. The camel was one of a pair owned by George Getz, owner of Lakewood Farm and Zoo. Getz, a Chicago coal magnate, was a major benefactor for the Holland fair, which was held where the south portion of Pilgrim Home Cemetery is located. Shortly after the fair, Getz shipped the camels to a charity fair at the South Shore Country Club in Chicago. One of the camels died en route and the other was placed in the Lincoln Park Zoo. The skin and skeleton of the dead camel were given to the Field Museum of Natural History in Chicago, and are still a part of the research collection.

Three
BEAUTIFUL ERA
BLOSSOMS
(1920–1940)

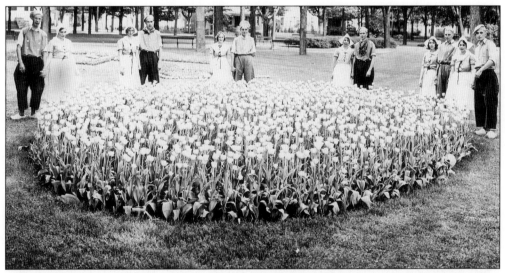

When Tulip Time was held for the first time in 1929, thousands of visitors viewed 100,000 tulips. Planted in 1928 on the suggestion of Mayor Earnest Brooks, these bulbs provided the city's first blossoms. Additional bulbs were planted in the fall of 1929, and Tulip Time was held May 13 through 17, 1930. On the festival's first day *The Holland Evening Sentinel's* banner headline read: "Tulip Reigns as Queen in City." The *Chicago Tribune's* James O'Donnell Bennett informed readers that 50,000 tulips were blossoming in Holland's Centennial Park. The tulip beds attracted these six couples attired in Dutch costumes. They stood behind one of the beds while other beds were in the shapes of a wooden shoe and windmill. Thousands more blossoms were planted on narrow strips of grass adjacent to the curb between the sidewalk and street on Twelfth and Nineteenth Streets. Holland High School biology students, led by their teacher Miss Lida Rogers, exhibited 6,000 tulips highlighting the school colors; maroon blossoms formed a background for a large orange H on the high school lawn. In a speech given to the Holland Woman's Literary Club April 27, 1927, Miss Rogers suggested that Holland hold an annual "Tulip Day." The festival itself began two years later.

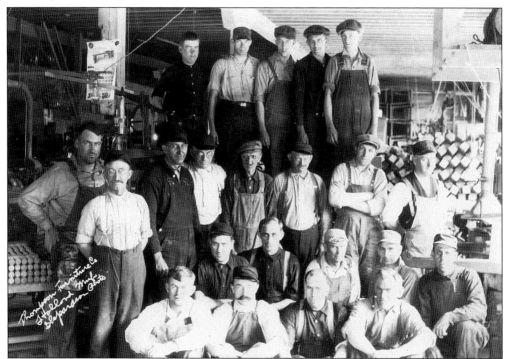

One of Holland's several furniture factories was the Thompson Manufacturing Company at 169-187 East Twelfth Street. These employees made bent wood closet tanks and seats, art mission specialties, and bungalow furniture. Its products were sold nationwide. Other furniture establishments in the 1920s included Charles P. Limbert, Ottawa Furniture, West Michigan Furniture, Holland Furniture, Bay View Furniture, and the Bush and Lane Piano Company.

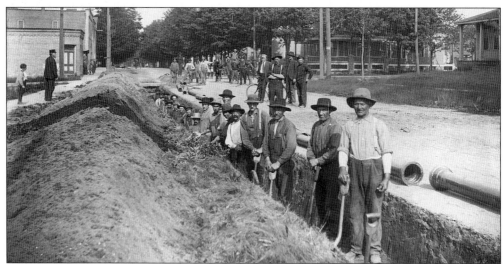

These Holland city employees are digging a water line on West Tenth Street, just west of Maple Avenue. The Anton Seif Brewery is at left, on the northeast corner. The building on the corner is presently occupied by the Ebenezer Asambleas de Dios (Assemblies of God) Church. The congregation built a new church on the property in 1993. The last factory on the property was Holland Wire Products, established in 1948.

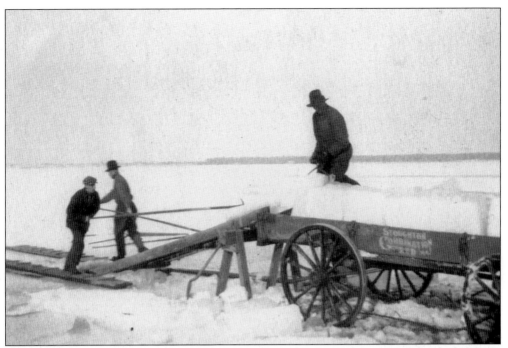

Ice was harvested March 7, 1921 on Black (Macatawa) Lake for use in Holland ice boxes. E. Lugers is at left. A. Neerken, on the right, is pushing the ice to the wagon. Adrian Heneveld is on the wagon putting cakes of ice in place. They are working at Jenison Park, a block east of Easter Marina. The location is now the home of the Tiara Yachts Corporate Yachting Center on Lakeway Drive.

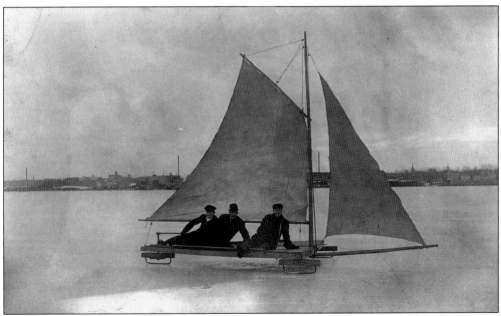

Sailing across Black Lake (officially named Lake Macatawa on June 4, 1935) was fast and popular in the 1920s. Ice boat racing drew large crowds to the frozen lake.

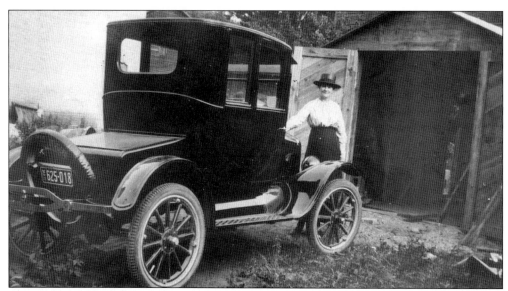

Miss Nellie Churchford, following a year of tent meetings, founded the Holland Rescue Mission in 1903. She was given a Model A Ford in 1928. She had previously conducted her evangelistic meetings on horseback. During the 1920s, Miss Churchford held baptisms of converts in Black Lake, at the foot of Tenth Street off the present site of Kollen Park. The baptisms followed tent meetings in a vacant lot at 54 West Eighth Street, site of *The Holland Sentinel* in 1928. Holland residents built a City Mission building for Miss Churchford in 1927. She died on December 6, 1931, at age 57. About 2,500 people attended her funeral, including some local masons, carpenters, and plasterers who had donated their labor to build the mission building.

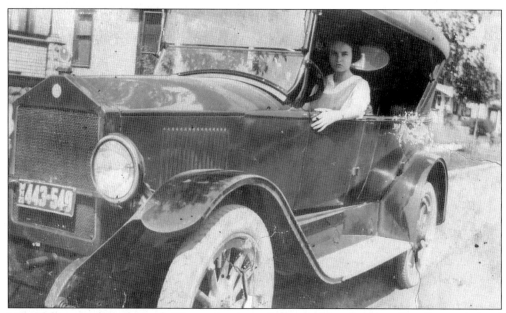

Mrs. William H. (Kitty) Vande Water, daughter of Mr. and Mrs. Anthony Van Ry, sits behind the wheel of a Ford parked in front of her parents' home at 201 West Fifteenth Street in the 1920s. During that decade, as automobiles became popular and the chief mode of transportation, both women and men learned to drive.

Constructed in 1892 of Waverly stone quarried east of Holland, the Tower Clock is a famed downtown landmark and best-known Waverly stone edifice. Located at 190 River Avenue on the northwest corner of River Avenue and Eighth Street, it presently houses a gift shop, Tower Clock Accents. The building was constructed to house the Holland City Bank. It has experienced several changes and renovations.

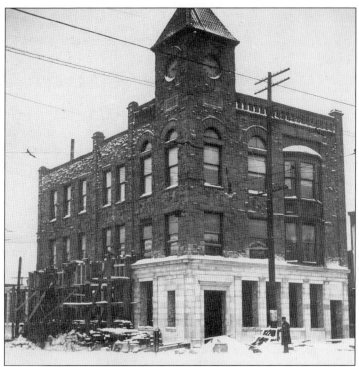

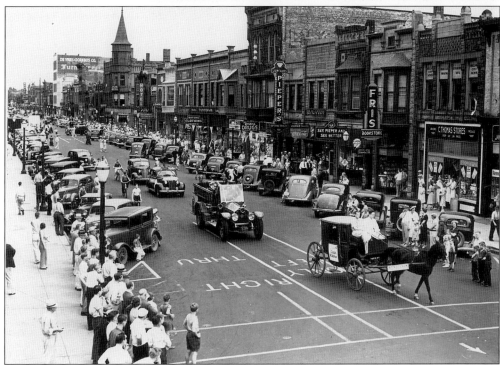

In August of 1938, as the Depression was winding down, Holland held a parade on Eighth Street. The parade was named Sales Mean Jobs, a promotion to provide jobs. One of the city's fire engines is preceded by a horse and carriage labeled "Dutch Kitchen."

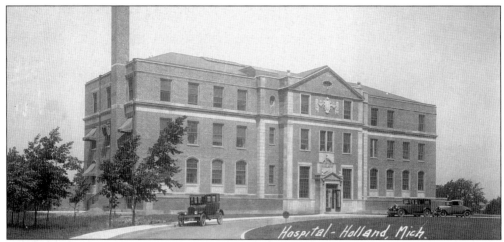

Holland Community Hospital opened on January 21, 1928. Located at 602 Michigan Avenue on the corner of Twenty-fourth Street and Michigan Avenue, the facility has been honored as "one of the nation's 10 most wired hospitals" and recognized for its use of technology in patient data and clinical communication. The 213-bed private hospital offers patient and outpatient services, including surgery, obstetrics, oncology, pediatrics, cardiology, geriatrics, psychiatric services, 24-hour emergency care, and a walk-in urgent care clinic. The hospital operates two pain clinics, a sleep disorders lab, a mammography center, a home care program, a substance abuse unit, and parish and school nursing programs. The hospital also has a $10 million Lakeshore Medical Campus on Holland's north side. The community had its first hospital in a home at 8 East Twelfth Street in 1917. In 1925, the Board of Public Works decided a hospital should be built and owned by the city. Between 1926 and 1929 the hospital was paid for with BPW profits which totaled $183,970.40. The hospital cost was $183,882.88. The first addition was made in 1948 and several additions have followed. About 15 years ago, voters from Holland and the townships of Park, Holland, and Laketown approved a private, non-governmental, not-for-profit corporation which permitted the hospital to enter other joint ventures.

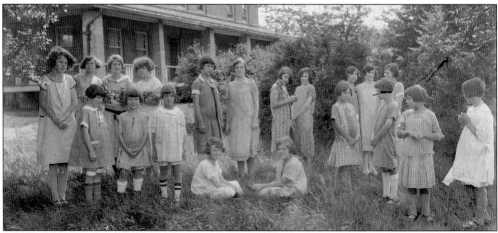

On September 20, 1924, the Sunnycrest School for Girls opened in the George A. Poole mansion at 958 South Shore Drive. Founded by Miss Helen Clark and supported by "Tag Days" and Holland businessmen, Sunnycrest helped 15 young girls who were orphans or had only one parent. From Chicago, Poole was a printer of railroad tickets. He built the home in 1906. The school closed shortly before World War II. It is now a private residence called Windy Ridge.

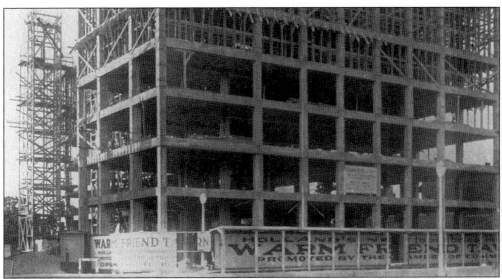

The Warm Friend Tavern inaugural banquet was held on April 30, 1925. Constructed by the Holland Furnace Company, the hotel's name was taken from the company's motto: "Holland Furnaces Make Warm Friends." Excavation began April 10, 1924 and contractor Frank Dyke was told to build the six-floor hotel in 300 days. Painting and decorating took 46 days. Located at 9 East Eighth Street, the hotel had 144 rooms with telephones, 100 with baths, on 4 floors. A grill, dining room, kitchen, and lobby were on the first floor. A barbershop was in the basement and, following the repeal of Prohibition, a Bier (Beer) Kelder was added. The sixth floor was used for social functions, including an elevated orchestra loft and later a private Tavern Club. After the demise of the furnace company, the hotel, with the exception of liquor licenses, was sold to Jack Vannette. Remodeling occurred in 1967 and 1979, and Vannette sold the building to Resthaven Patrons, Inc. on December 10, 1981. Operated by Resthaven, the building serves as a retirement home for senior citizens.

Dimnent Memorial Chapel stands on Twelfth Street and College Avenue on the Hope College campus. In addition to college religious and secular services, the 1,300-seat facility is used for community functions. Dedicated June 7, 1929, during the annual meeting of the General Synod of the Reformed Church in America, Hope Memorial Chapel's cornerstone was laid October 12, 1927. On August 14, 1959, the college's Board of Trustees named the chapel in honor of Dr. Edward D. Dimnent, who served as Hope College President from 1918 to 1931. Dimnent died on July 4, 1959. This picture shows construction of the 120-foot tower, which is the dominant structure on the campus.

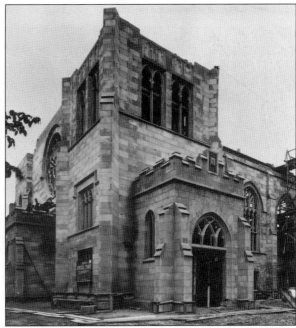

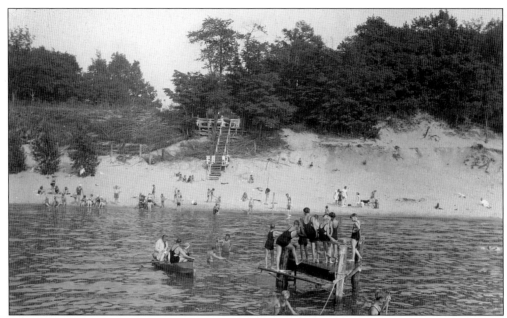

When boys and men went swimming in the 1920s and early 1930s, they were required to wear shoulder straps on bathing suits. These people are participants at a Boy Scout camp on Lake Michigan, north of Ottawa Beach. Arrests were made, including some publicized in 1932, which cited a state regulation: "If men's bodies were bared to the waist or the straps of bathing suits dangled over the shoulders," violators would be charged with disorderly conduct and indecent exposure.

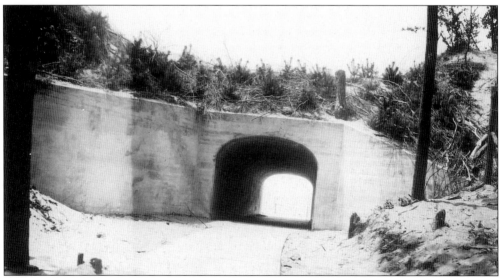

In 1928, Ottawa County accepted a property trade offer from Lakewood Farm and Zoo owner George Getz. It gave the county a 200-foot stretch of land and lakefront property in exchange for 66 feet of highway adjoining Lakewood Farm. Originally called Getz Park, the 14-foot-wide concrete tunnel was cut through the sand dune in August 1929. On July 5, 1929 the Ottawa County Road Commission suggested the name Arcade Park, believing the word tunnel denoted gloom. After additional discussion, the name Tunnel Park prevailed.

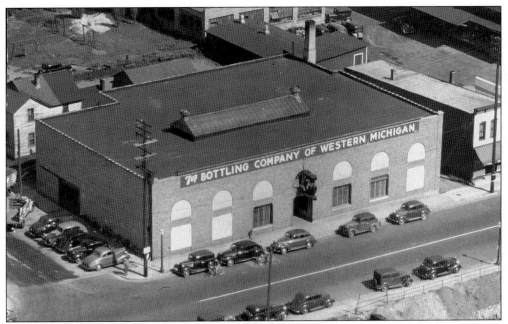

The *7up* Bottling Company of Western Michigan was founded in 1934 by Phillips Brooks. In 1940, the building was on Fourth Street and River Avenue and stayed in that location until moving to the Southside Industrial Park in Holland more than 35 years ago.

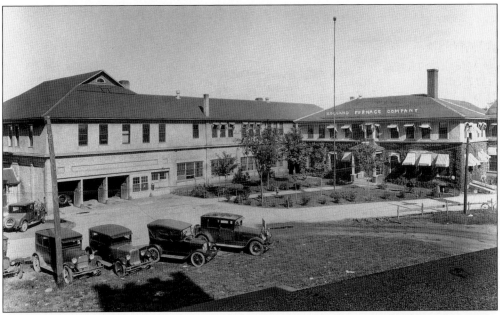

The Holland Furnace Company began operations in 1906. Residing in Holland for 60 years, the company came to Holland under the Bonus Plan which gave firms a property incentive to settle and build there. In the early 1920s, the expanding company, which at one time was the largest furnace company in the nation, built a new office building and gymnasium. It was located on Columbia Avenue, near 20th Street. To the left was the Holland YMCA building that the furnace used as a dock.

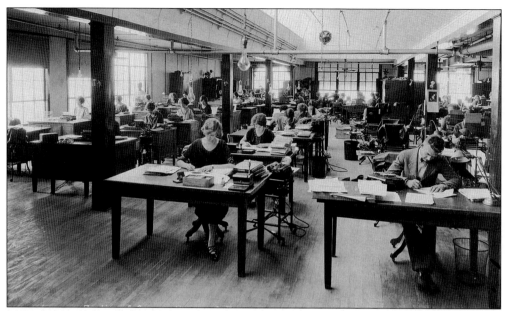

The accounting and bookkeeping departments of the Holland Furnace Company were located in a building constructed in the early 1920s. Earl Van Lente (right) was one of four people killed July 28, 1928, when a speedboat they were riding in collided with the Goodrich steamer *City of Holland* bound for Chicago. The 30-foot speedboat was piloted by Paul Landwehr, the 20-year-old son of Mr. and Mrs. A.H. Landwehr. He perished in the crash along with 14-year-old John Kolla Nystrom and 32-year-old Johannes (John) Arens of Holland, who left a wife and four children. Landwehr was the son of the company co-founder and Nystrom was the grandson of company co-founder John Kolla.

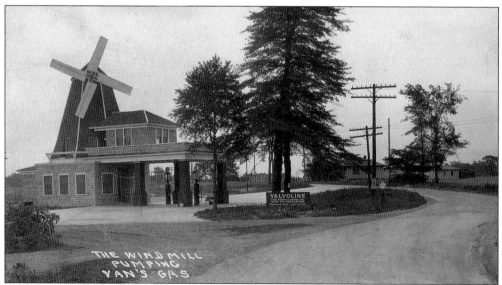

The Windmill Station stood on the corner of 32nd Street and 160th Avenue. Demolished in 2000, the building had been built in 1926 by the Vandenberg Brothers Oil Company at 1649 West 32nd Street. The station pumped Van's gas. Now 64th Street, the road was known in 1926 as the West Michigan Pike, stretching from Holland to Chicago.

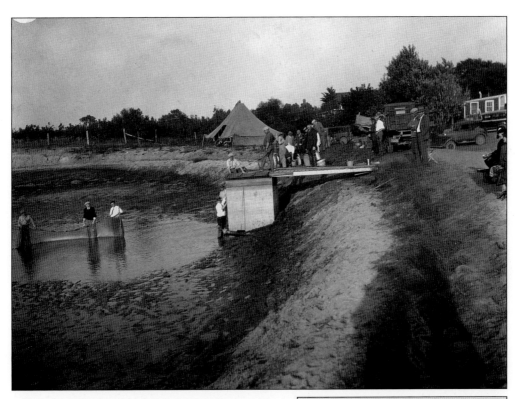

In 1935, members of the Holland Fish and Game Club covered the water and used a net to remove bass from the club's pond on M-21 between Holland and Zeeland. Thousands of these fish were then planted in Lake Macatawa. That same year, club members were also netting tons of fish from the inland lake. Netting took place in the early spring in Pine Creek Bay or the Big Bayou and fish were shipped to fish markets in large cities, including New York and Chicago.

On May 15, 1937, Robert Vande Water flew his red, two-seat, open cockpit biplane over Holland and dropped tulips on the Holland City Hall to open the tulip festival. The tulips were attached to tiny parachutes and dropped in honor of Mayor Henry Geerlings and city officials. Vande Water stands at the Park Township Airport on Ottawa Beach Road, about five miles west of Holland. The 80-acre airport site was purchased in 1936 by Park Township for $30,000, which included $24,500 from the WPA (Works Progress Administration). Dedication of the new facility during Tulip Time featured an air show. One visitor was drug store proprietor Charles R. Walgreen, who arrived in his twin-motor Lockheed.

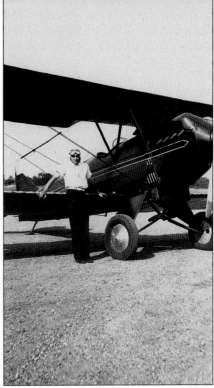

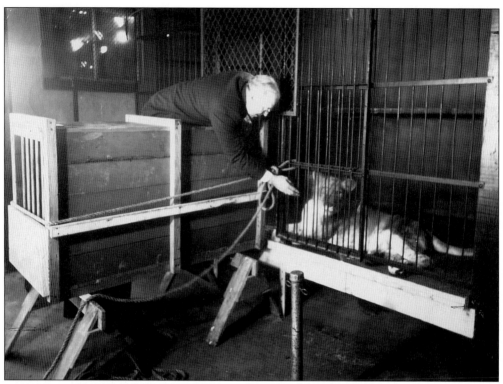

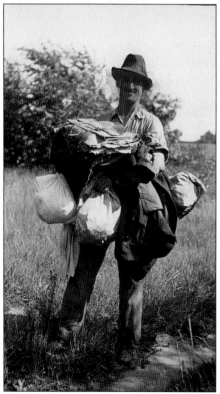

On October 25, 1933, George F. Getz announced he was closing Lakewood Farm and Zoo, and the animals were transferred to Chicago's new Brookfield Zoo. Caged animals, such as lion Ri Ri, coaxed by manager Andrew Peterson, were transported by truck. Making the trip were 1,241 mammals, including lions, tigers, leopards, monkeys, polar bears, deer, an elephant, a hippopotamus, a rhinoceros, 15 reptiles, and 201 birds. One bird, a cockatoo, is still living at the zoo. Nancy, the elephant, was driven to her new home in a trailer, and state police escorts from Michigan, Indiana, and Illinois met the trailer at each state line. The pythons, 28 and 30 feet long, were shipped in heated boxes. Getz opened his farm in 1910 and the zoo in 1913.

Hoboes began arriving in Holland as the nation moved into the 20th Century. These tramps rode the freight trains and stayed in the areas north of the depot and near the Waverly railroad yard. Others camped in wooded places near Black River in a section that became Windmill Island in 1965, and where Freedom Village is today. Often these hoboes, such as this 1930s tramp, asked for small jobs in return for food. Hoboes left the area in the late 1930s.

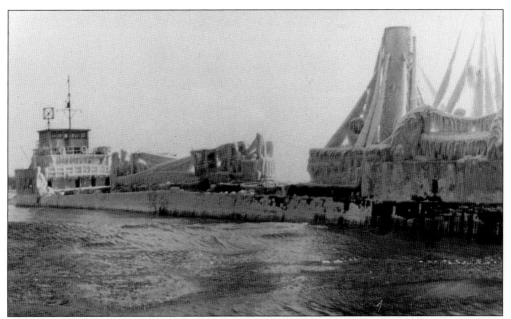

On December 6, 1936, 24 sailors were rescued in 14-degree temperatures off the 286-foot freighter *Burlington*. During a heavy storm in Lake Michigan, the ship smashed into a sandbar 400 feet off Ottawa Beach and ran aground. The mishap left a jagged V-shaped split near the center of the hold. While buried in the sand, the ship's cargo of 2,217 tons of pig iron was removed. Ice completely covered the ship, which sat mired north of the north breakwater. Attempts to re-float the ship failed and it broke up and eventually sank. In recent years, scuba divers have recovered a few pig iron ingots left behind.

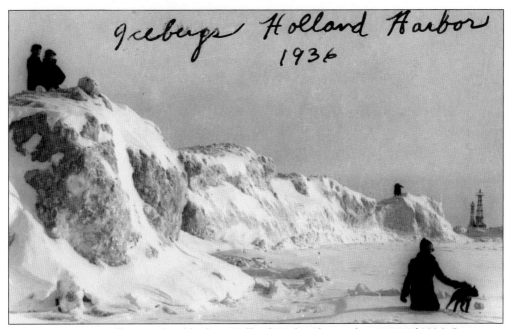

Icebergs were especially rugged and high at Holland Harbor during the winter of 1936. Spectators liked to climb the snow-covered icebergs to view the end of the pier and Lake Michigan.

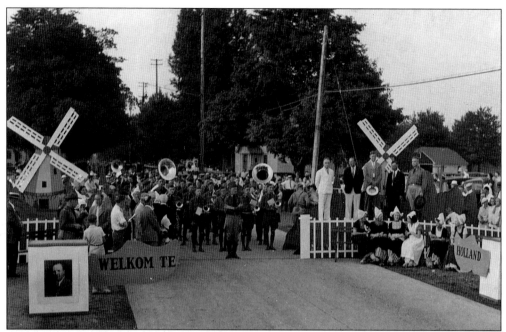

A crowd of 3,500 people attended the dedication of US-31A in Holland August 11, 1936. Army soldiers and airplanes, as well as the 121st Field Artillery Band, entertained on Michigan Avenue just south of Twenty-eighth Street. The road consisted of 8.3 miles of paved concrete and became the new highway between Holland and Saugatuck, now called Blue Star Highway. With the 120-foot right of way, the highway had a 62-foot grade and a 20-foot concrete pavement.

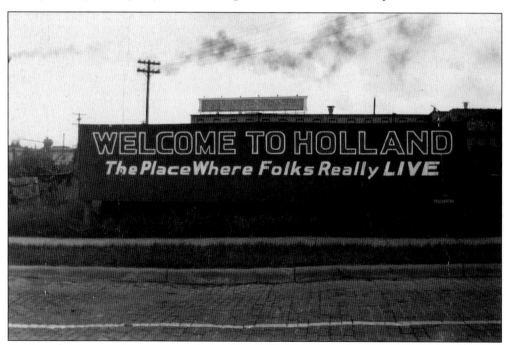

Residents, visitors, and tourists were greeted by this sign prior to World War II. It was displayed on the cobblestoned Pine Avenue, near Seventh Street.

Four

WAR, VICTORY,
AND BEYOND

(1940–1970)

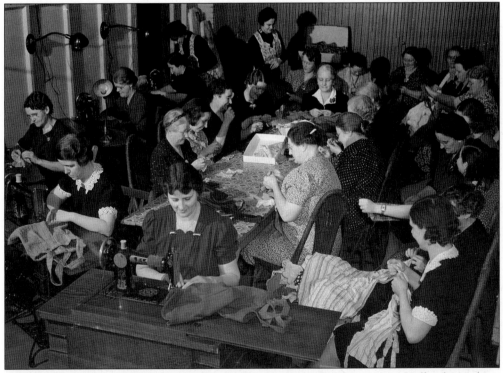

On Christmas Eve in 1940, women of the Salvation Army Home League in Holland were busy sewing clothing for European refugee children, the victims of Nazi Germany, in a war that started September 1, 1939. Three cartons of clothing had been sent to London, England where the Salvation Army cared for thousands of refugee children. Included in the cartons were 100 pairs of mittens, 30 skirts and sweaters, 50 baby garments, quilts, boys' pants, shirts, and overalls. The league also spent time making and fixing clothing for Netherlands residents.

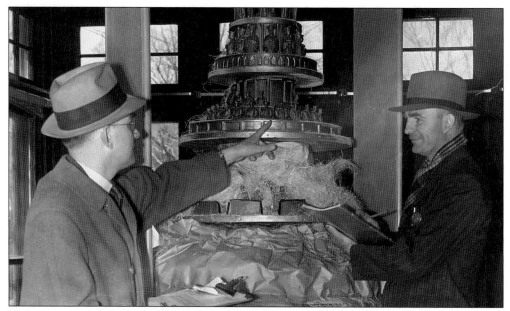

A clock was featured in the Netherlands exhibit of the New York World's Fair in 1939. It arrived in Holland April 10, 1940, and was placed in the Netherlands Museum. Museum director Willard C. Wichers (left) and U.S. Collector of Customs H.R. Walker unwrap the timepiece. Wichers is pointing at the clock's moving parts. The clock is now featured in the Holland Museum.

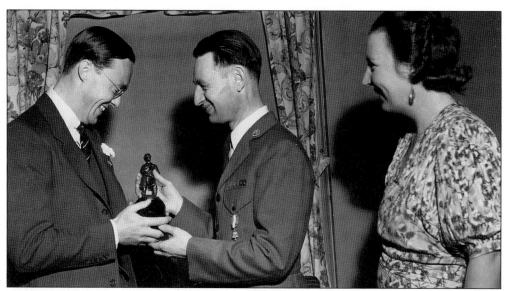

Prince Bernhard of the Netherlands received a Boy Scout statue from William H. Vande Water on June 9, 1941 during the Dutch royal couple's first visit to Holland. When Vande Water interviewed the prince for *The Grand Rapids Press*, Bernhard noted a Boy Scout pin on Vande Water's coat. Following conversation about scouting and the exchange of the international Boy Scout handclasp, Vande Water arranged for the statue presentation. Vande Water was a district commissioner for the Ottawa-Allegan Boy Scout Council and wore his uniform. During the same visit, Princess Juliana (right) was honored at Hope College with an honorary degree marking the college's 75th anniversary.

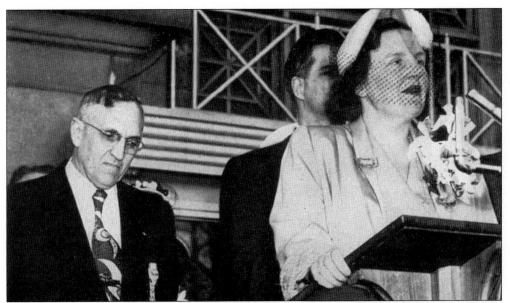

Princess Juliana became queen in 1948 when her mother, Queen Wilhelmina, who had reigned for 50 years, abdicated. Juliana, the new queen of the Netherlands, returned to the town of Holland on April 16, 1952 and spoke in front of the City Hall. The royal couple recalled their 1941 visit to Holland. Stationed in England as an officer in the Allied Forces, Prince Bernhard had not seen his wife for a year. Knowing the princess had been invited to Holland, and because of World War II he was staying in Canada, the prince arranged to surprise his wife. The couple rendezvoused in the Warm Friend Tavern.

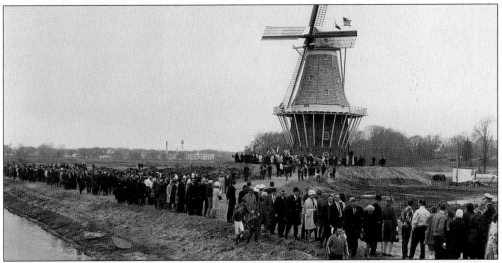

Hundreds of Holland residents and visiting dignitaries attended the dedication of *Windmill De Zwaan* and Windmill Island on April 10, 1965. Prince Bernhard of the Netherlands participated in the ceremony along with Michigan Governor George Romney. Dutch milwright, Jan Diederik Medendorp of the Netherlands, restored the 200-year-old historic windmill. He had dismantled it near Vinkel for the sea voyage to the United States. The ship arrived in Muskegon and the mill parts were trucked to Holland. The prince presented Mayor Nelson Bosman with a bottle of water from the river that flowed past the mill in the Netherlands.

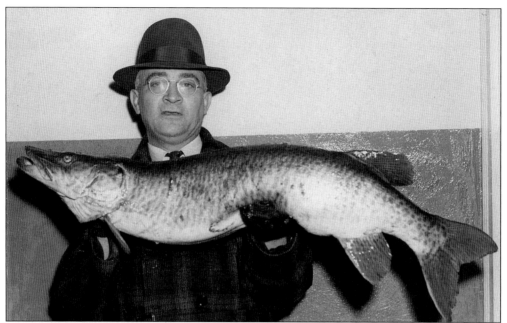

Jack Vander Ploeg of Holland speared this muskellunge in Lake Macatawa on February 28, 1945. The "muskie" weighed 48 pounds and was 54 inches long. Fishing in a tent on the ice of the Big Bayou, Vander Ploeg used a silver minnow for a lure. *The Holland Evening Sentinel* said: "The minnow was tied on a string to the tent where he fished; the tent, blowing in the wind, caused the minnow to move."

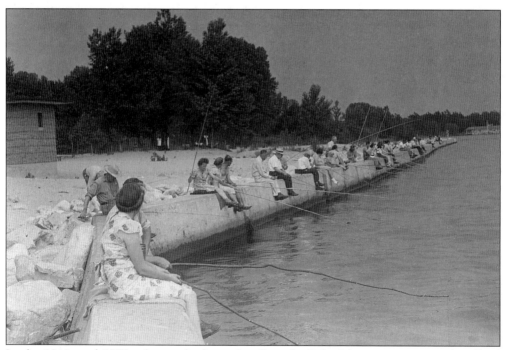

In the 1940s and 1950s, the north channel wall in the Lake Macatawa portion of Holland Harbor attracted men and women to fish using bamboo poles and long branches and sticks.

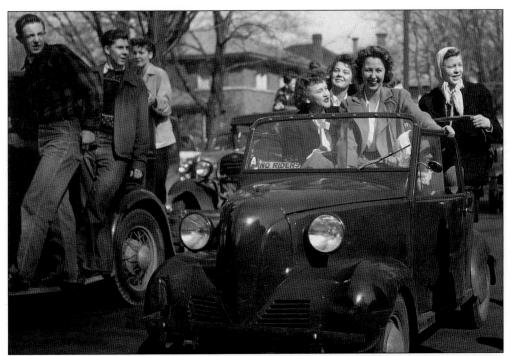

These Holland High School students enjoyed a spring day and the school's state championship game in the Michigan Class A State Basketball Tournament. On March 31, 1946, Arlene Poll drove her Crosley car with passengers Elaine Brower, Betty Gilcrest, Carol Houtman, and Esther Huyser. The boys riding on the running board of the other car are Robert (Bud) Miedema and Eugene Van Dyke.

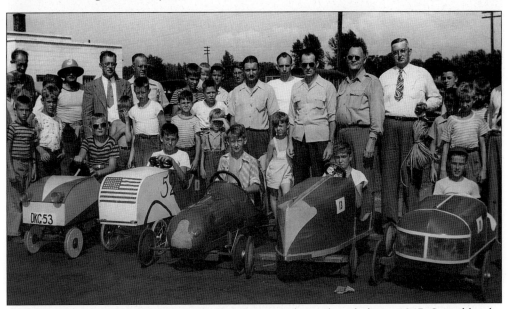

Dave Rumsey (center) of Holland won the Centennial soap box derby in 1947. Staged by the Kiwanis Club, it was held August 13 on the Columbia Avenue hill at 20th Street. The event was one of several highlights as Holland marked its 100th anniversary.

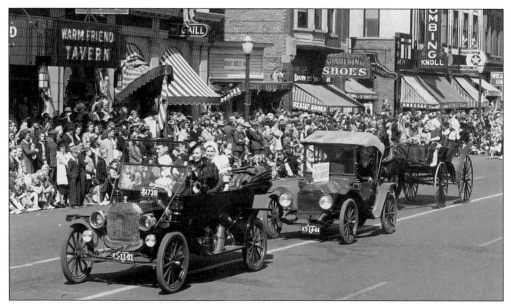

More than 25,000 people watched Holland's Centennial Parade on August 14, 1947. Vintage autos and a horse and buggy composed one division. Four bands were interspersed between church floats tracing the city's religious growth, choral groups singing Dutch psalms, ox-drawn wagons, along with historic fire engines and an 1871 hand pumper.

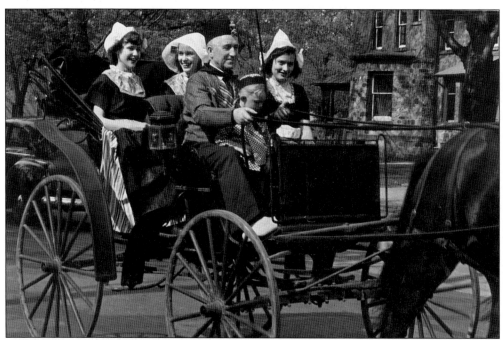

Hub Boone, whose family operated a livery, feed, and stables company in the 19th Century and first quarter of the 20th Century, drove this buggy with four Dutch-costumed Holland residents during the 1947 Centennial Parade. The livery was located on Seventh Street and Central Avenue, about five blocks south of where the horse and buggy are pictured. In the background is a portion of Holland's first hospital, built as a private residence by Dr. Henry Kremers.

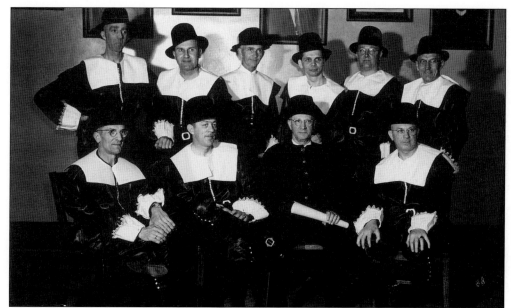

To observe the 1947 Centennial, Holland's City Council was decked out in costumes, similar to those the town officials would have worn in the Netherlands a century before. Pictured, from left to right, are the following: (seated) Fred Galien, William Meengs, Mayor Ben Steffens, Henry Te Roller; (standing) John Bontekoe, Bernard De Pree, Herman Mooi, Melvin Van Tatenhove, Edward Prins, and Harry Harrington.

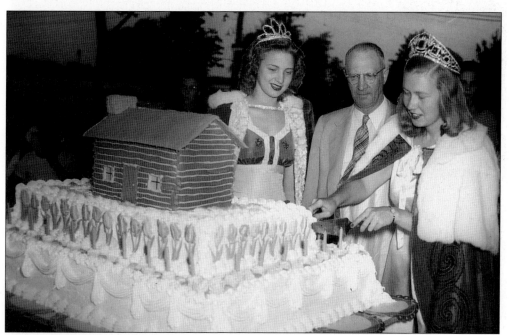

Miss Holland, Sally Diekema, cut the first piece of cake served at the Centennial picnic held in Kollen Park. The 300-pound, two-tiered cake featured a bottom tier, 3 by 4 feet, on the top of a chocolate-frosted replica of the first log cabin church. Watching are Miss Columbia, LaVerne Huyser and Mayor Ben Steffens. More than 10,000 people attended.

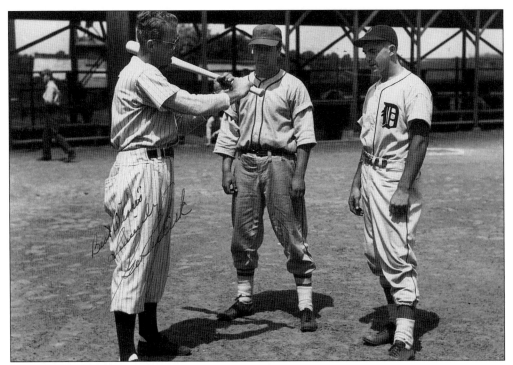

The Holland Flying Dutchmen were a popular semi-professional baseball team. Starting in 1934, the Dutchmen played until the mid-1950s. Opponents were the famed Negro League teams including the Kansas City Monarchs, the Atlanta Black Crackers, and the Chicago American Giants, plus the bearded House of David teams. In 1948, former New York Yankee outfielder George Selkirk held tryouts for Holland players at Riverview Park. The players pictured here are Clyde Kehrwecker and Frank Wlodarcyzk, wearing a former Detroit Tigers home uniform. In 1946, the Dutchmen purchased the 1945 world championship uniforms worn by the Tigers.

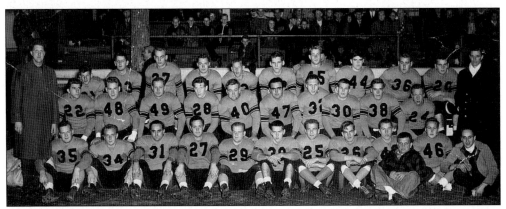

From 1947 through 1949, the Holland Hurricanes played football in the Michigan Independent Football League. Organized and operated the first two years by Fred Bocks, the Holland Lions club took over the club in 1949. Home games were played at Riverview Park and more than 4,000 people attended the first game. In addition to ex-Holland High School and Hope College players, the Hurricanes had high school and ex-collegiate players from Grand Haven and Zeeland. They fielded a 30-member unit and games were against Benton Harbor, Grand Rapids, Detroit, Jackson, Ann Arbor, Flint, and Highland Park.

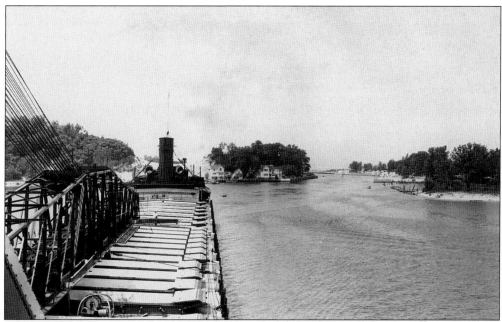

A Great Lakes freighter enters Lake Macatawa after clearing the Holland Harbor channel in the early 1950s.

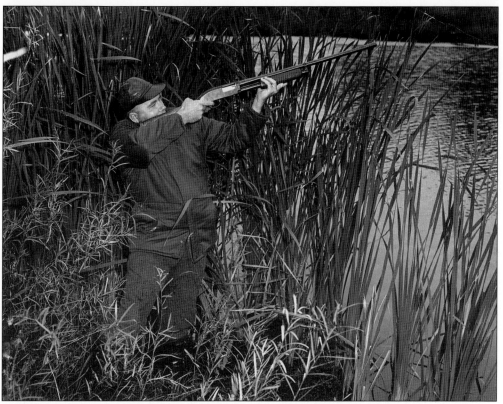

A duck hunter takes aim in the Black River marsh more than 40 years ago.

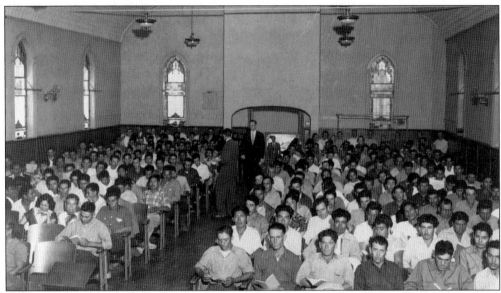

This is a group of braceros attending a work session at the South Olive Christian Reformed Church at 6200 120th Avenue, north of Holland, in the 1940s. After World War II these Mexican Nationals began picking cucumbers for the H.J. Heinz Company.

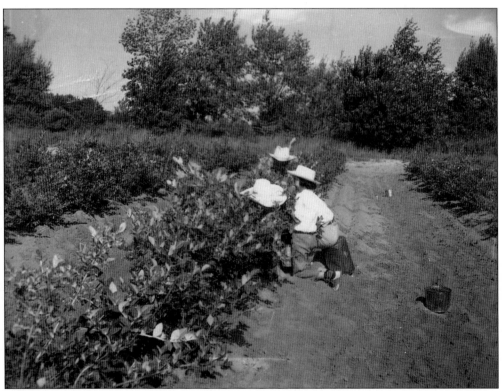

Migrant workers began picking cucumbers in Holland area fields following World War II. Blueberries were picked by all ages, including migrants and teenagers, when the bushes on the sandy soil needed harvesting in the early 1950s.

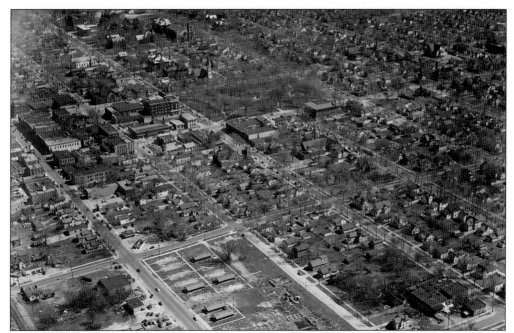

Holland opened its municipal recreational building on November 16, 1954. Called the Civic Center, (center foreground) the facility is located between Eighth and Ninth Streets on the north and south, and Pine and Maple Avenues on the east and west. A tannery occupied the site until the 1930s. Purchased by the city in 1941, the vacant lot housed quonset buildings for public housing in 1950. A city vote approved the facility in 1952.

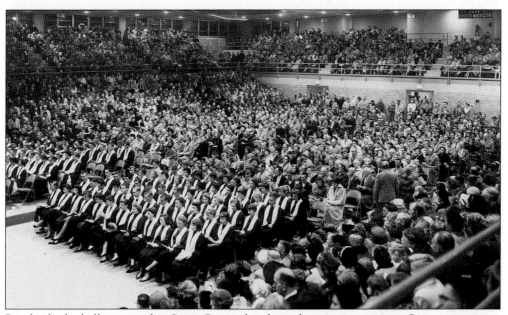

Besides basketball games, the Civic Center has hosted numerous events. Commencements, concerts, religious services, gem, mineral, home, and sports shows as well as Tulip Time activities have filled the facility. There are 994 theater seats upstairs. Capacity, with pulled out bleachers and seats on the main floor and stage, reaches 3,000.

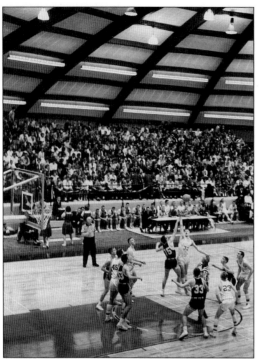

Holland High School's basketball team played its first game in the new domed fieldhouse January 27, 1962. The many spectators watched the Dutch lose to Traverse City, 57–45.

Semi-professional basketball, featuring ex-college and high school performers, entertained Holland area fans from 1958 through the early 1960s. Don Cook of Holland (standing, second from left) presented night basketball on Saturdays in the Zeeland High School gymnasium and the Holland Civic Center. The first game at the Civic Center drew 2,857 fans. Called Cook's Oilers, the home team was composed of former Big Ten conference team members, plus Hope College and Michigan Intercollegiate Athletic Association (MIAA) alumni, as well as Holland High and Holland Christian athletes. In 1964, a victory over the Grand Rapids Tackers gave the Oilers the Midwest Professional Basketball League Championship.

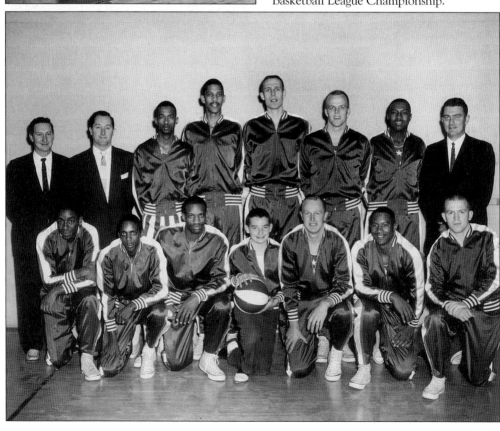

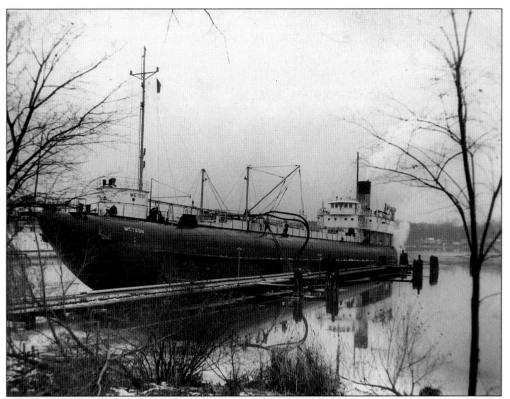

Meteor, a whaleback tanker, unloaded its cargo in 1948. The last of its type of United States registry, the ship frequently delivered gasoline for Holland residents.

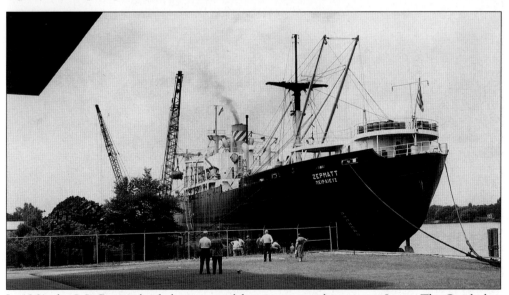

In 1961, the *S.S. Zermatt* loaded scrap metal for an overseas shipment to Japan. The Greek ship was docked at Harrington Coal Dock and carried compressed auto bodies to Japanese smelters. Misshapen girders, which went through the ship's hatches into the hold, were also on board. The *Zermatt* was one of the foreign ships that made Holland a port.

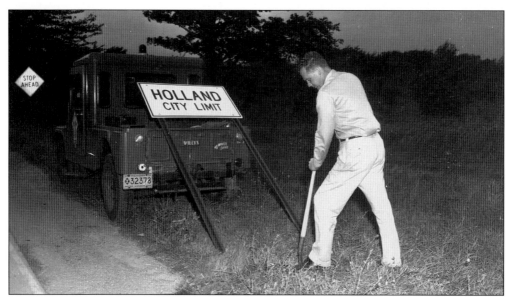

Holland extended its boundaries in 1958. The city's size and the school district were increased to six miles. Additional annexation occurred in later years.

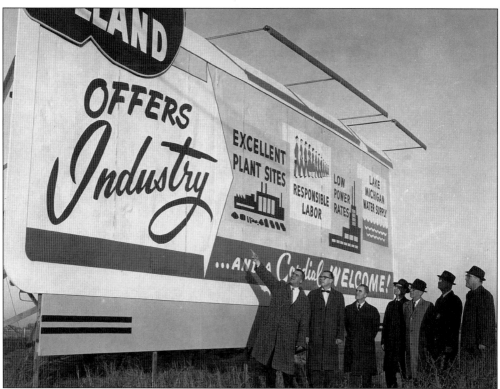

In 1962, the Holland Economic Development Corporation (HEDCOR) was started. The first project was the Southside Industrial Park. As the signage indicates, Holland offered excellent plant sites, responsible labor, lower power rates, and a Lake Michigan water supply. HEDCOR directors campaigned and raised $250,000 in 1963 for industrial development.

Five

DECADES OF DIVERSITY

(1970–2000)

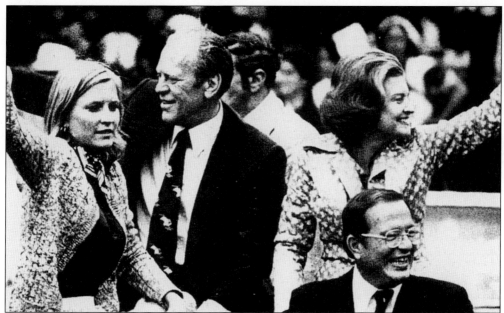

President Gerald R. Ford, former U.S. Congressman for Holland, Ottawa, and Kent Counties, rode in the 1976 Tulip Time Parade of Bands. It was the first time a president had ridden in a festival parade. Ford sat on an open automobile and was accompanied by his wife Betty, daughter Susan, and U.S. Rep. Guy Vander Jagt. In 1980, presidential hopefuls Ronald Reagan and George Bush rode in the same festival parade.

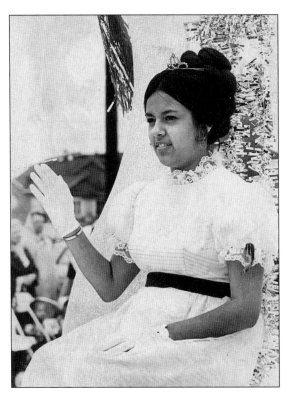

Thirty-seven years ago, the Latin Americans United for Progress began staging a May Fiesta during the first weekend in May. Selection of a queen was a fiesta feature. This young woman won the honor in 1970.

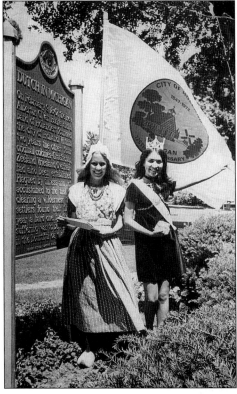

During Holland's 125th anniversary in July 1972, community representatives invited Michigan mayors to attend the play *Knickerbocker Holiday* at Hope College. The ambassadors were Dutch "Klompen" Dancer, Cindy Tamminga, and Estelita Saucedo, the LAUP queen. The girls posed in front of the *Dutch in Michigan* sign in Centennial Park, placed there by the Michigan State Historical Commission in 1957.

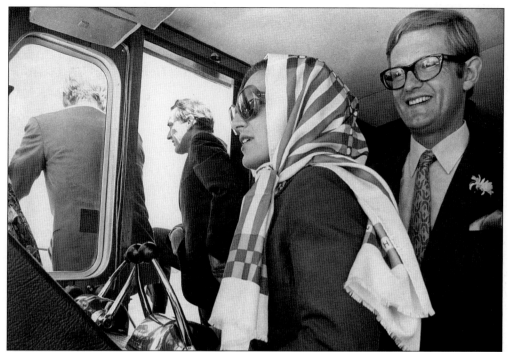

In September 1972, Princess Margriet and her husband Pieter visited the city of Holland for an observance of our town's 125th anniversary. The couple returned in October 1997 and participated in the dedication of two statues, as the community marked its 150th anniversary. In 1972, the princess piloted a yacht on Lake Macatawa while her husband watched.

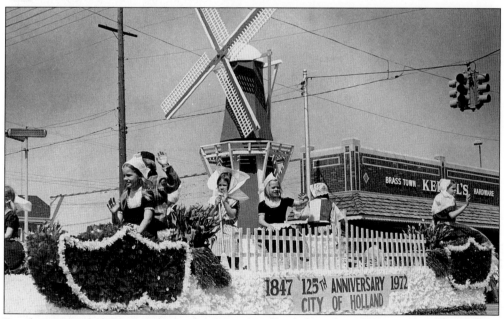

Dutch-costumed children rode on the City of Holland float during the August 1972 parade. Marking the community's 125th anniversary, the float featured a windmill and papier-mâché wooden shoes.

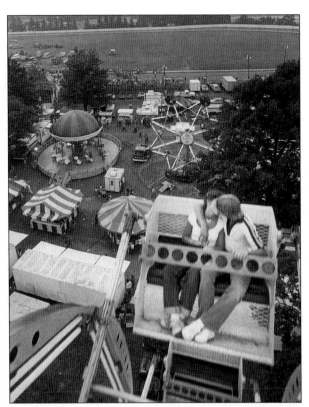

The Ottawa County Fair began in 1959. The Ferris wheel has always beckoned young lovers to kiss while at the top, like this couple in 1971.

Downtown Holland was torn up during the summer of 1974 as cement curbs and cutouts were placed on Eighth Street. When completed between River and College Avenues, parallel parking was permitted for vehicles arriving from the west. This traffic pattern was reversed in 1988.

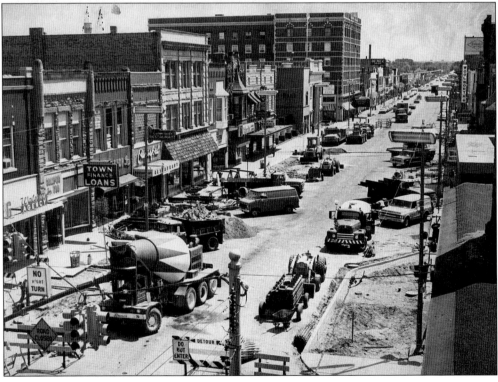

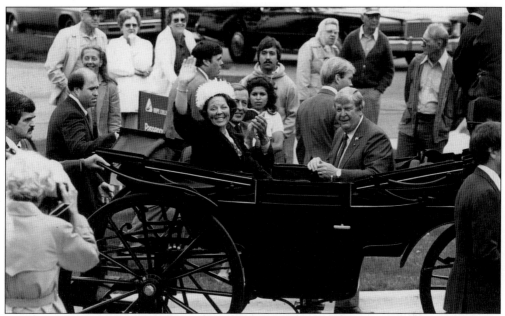

Queen Beatrix of the Netherlands visited Holland on June 26, 1982. The queen, accompanied by her husband Prince Claus and Holland Mayor Richard Smith, rode in a carriage through downtown to Hope College. In addition to speaking at a Hope convocation, the queen ate a picnic lunch with local residents in Kollen Park, sailed on Lake Macatawa on the U.S. Coast Guard ship *Acacia*, and also visited Windmill Island. She climbed the seven-story windmill her father had dedicated in 1965. The royal couple's visit to Holland was part of a nationwide tour marking 200 years of unbroken diplomatic ties between the U.S. and the Netherlands. Their first stop was in Washington, where President and Mrs. Ronald Reagan entertained the couple. In 1952, the queen's parents had made a similar visit to the White House, as guests of President and Mrs. Harry Truman.

Potential candidates chat with the 1991 Latin Americans United for Progress Fiesta Queen. Crowning of the queen has been the LAUP fiesta highlight since 1965.

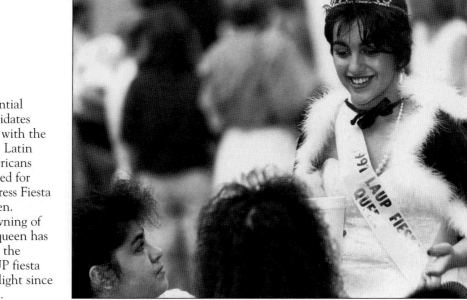

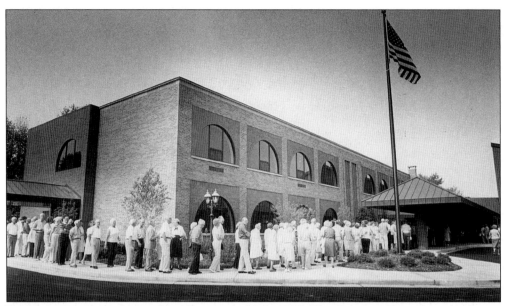

Evergreen Commons Senior Center opened in July 1985. The Center is located on the former site of Holland Christian High School and Middle School. These people are waiting to tour the Center on its opening day. The renovated building, including a wood shop, was formerly a middle school at 480 State Street. The Center has been enlarged and includes a swimming pool and exercise room.

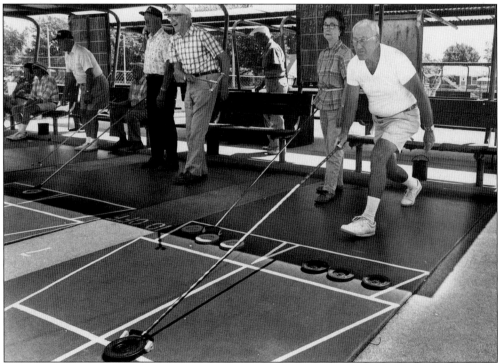

Holland seniors play shuffleboard at Moran Park on West 21st Street, one of the several city parks located throughout the city.

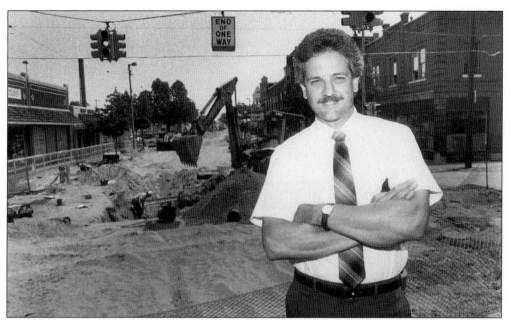

Greg Robinson, Main Street Director in 1988 and now Holland Assistant City Manager, handled the development of Snowmelt (above) and Streetscape. Eighth Street was torn up from 56 West Eighth Street, west of River Avenue, to 106 East Eighth Street, east of College Avenue. The two projects were constructed during the summer of 1988. Snowmelt provides an underground heated water system that keeps the Streetscape sidewalks and streets dry during snowfall.

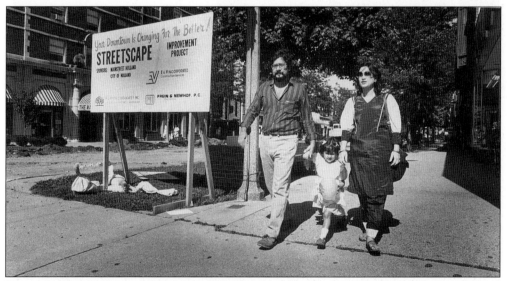

Trees, plantings, lighting, and brick walks constituted Streetscape. One-way traffic was directed from east to west with parallel parking. Statish Rawat (left), his wife Neelu, and four-year-old daughter, Avanti, shopped downtown during the August 1988 excavation.

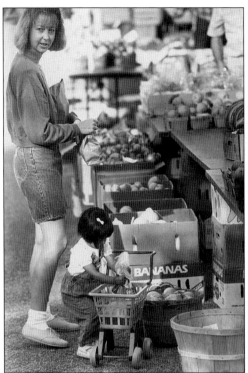

Farmers' Market operates in Holland's Civic Center parking lot Wednesdays and Saturdays from mid-May through mid-November. Farmers supply produce in the spring, summer, and fall seasons. Virginia Oakley received shopping assistance from her two-year-old daughter Sara during their September outing at the market.

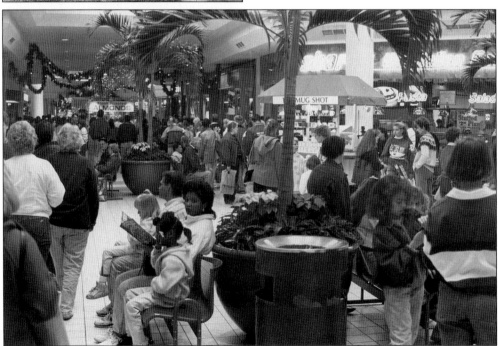

West Shore Mall, located at US-31 and James Street, was Holland's first mall. Constructed in 1987, the mall is frequently crowded. Adjacent property on the south houses an outlet mall, while the east and west sides of the highway and nearby intersecting streets are now filled with retail stores, which range from national chains to locally-owned operations.

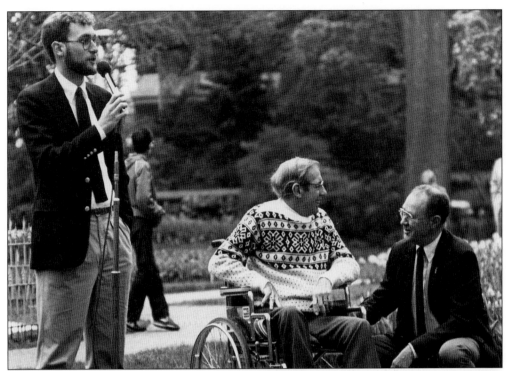

Brick pathways were added to Centennial Park in 1987. Holland residents purchased the bricks in a buy-a-brick campaign. Councilman and future mayor Philip Tanis (left) spearheaded the program. Forrest Fynewever (center) suggested the program. Mayor William A. Sikkel is kneeling.

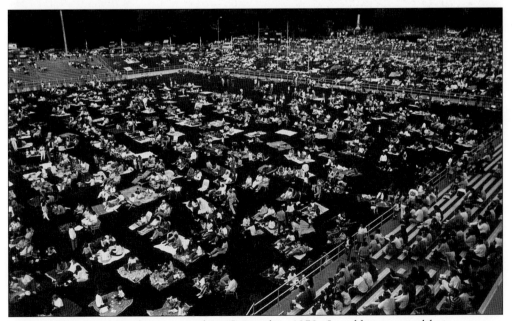

Holland Municipal Stadium opened in September 1979. In addition to athletic contests, commencements, and concerts, the stadium lawn, bleachers, and grassy berm provide spaces for people to watch the annual Fourth of July fireworks.

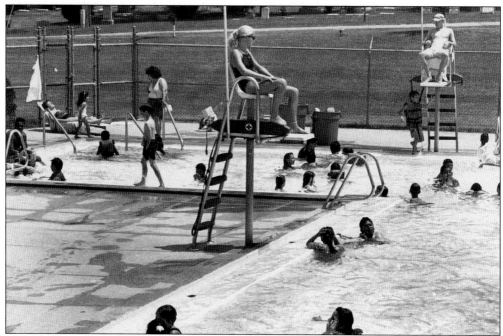

Because of the generosity of J. Russel Bouws, Holland youngsters enjoy hours of summertime fun in the city pool. The founder of Russ' Restaurants donated funds and the pool was constructed in 1973. Bouws Pool is located west of Pilgrim Home Cemetery on East 16th Street near Fairbanks Avenue.

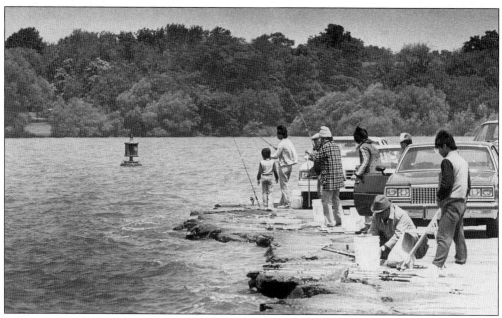

Fishing off Kollen Park in Lake Macatawa continues to be popular with all generations at various times of the year.

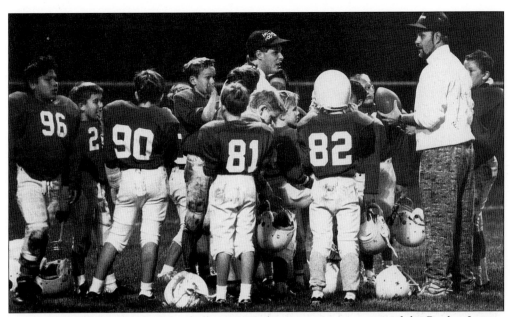

Learning the fundamentals of football occupies these youngsters as part of the Rocket League competition. The boys are dressed in equipment, comparable to their older counterparts.

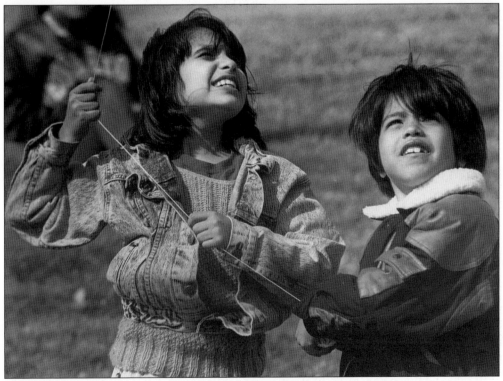

March spring breezes bring out the challenge of kite flying. Tugging on the string and trying to keep the kite under control are Holland youngsters Esperanza Morales and Pablo Cazares.

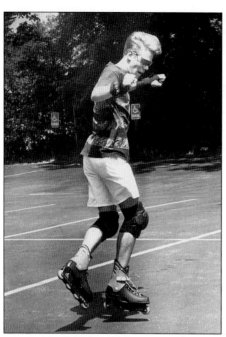

For more than a decade, roller blading has been wildly popular among people of all ages.

Lake Macatawa, with its varied breezes, attracts windsurfers to these waters near the Holland State Park campground.

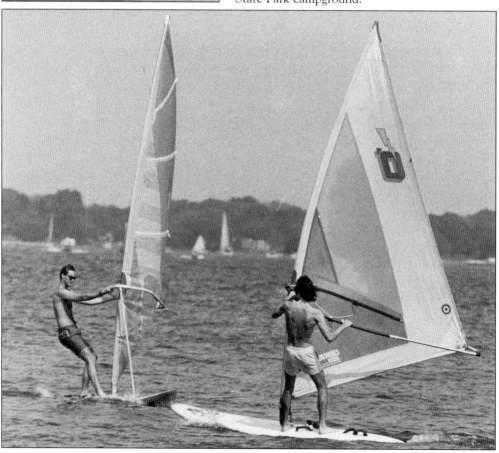

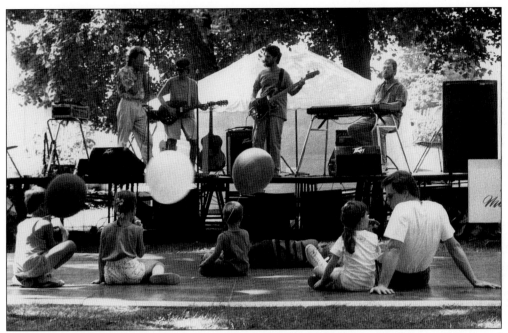

Summertime instrumental and vocal entertainment draws children and adults to Centennial Park. Several concerts are performed between Memorial Day and Labor Day, when Holland enjoys an influx of tourists and resorters.

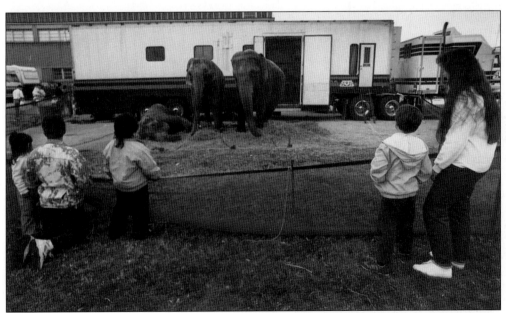

All ages are excited when the circus "comes to town." Prior to performing at the Civic Center, these elephants are presenting some pre-show action while outside their trailer in the building's parking lot.

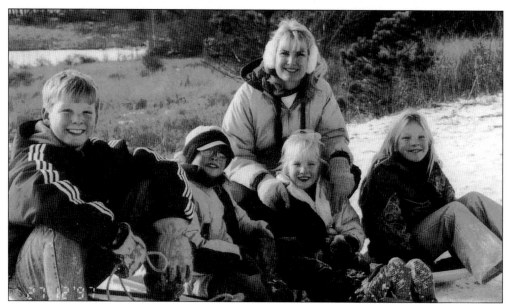

Van Raalte Farm, originally the residence of Ben Van Raalte, was purchased by the city in 1983 for $350,000 from Van Raalte family heirs. Ben Van Raalte was the son of the city's founder and built the homestead on a hill after the Civil War. The farm added the sledding hill in the mid-1990s. Enjoying the facilities are Nancy Sivertson and her children Jonathan, Kristina, Sarah, and Marissa Padding (wearing hat). Portions of the area were formerly working farms. The farm is between East 16th and East 24th Streets. The eastern lot line is Country Club Road.

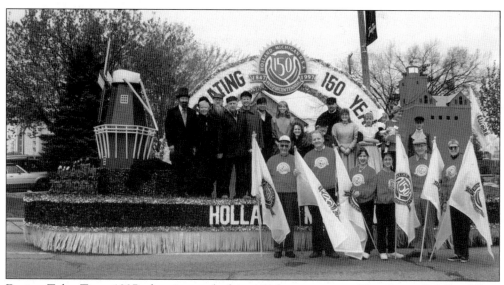

During Tulip Time 1997, the city marked its 150th anniversary. The City of Holland float carried descendants of the original settlers. The float featured miniatures of the tourist attraction *Windmill De Zwaan* and "Big Red," the name given the lighthouse on the south channel wall in Holland Harbor. Painted red in 1956 and acquired from the U.S. Coast Guard in 1978, the lighthouse belongs to the Holland Harbor Lighthouse Historical Commission. Members of the Sesquicentennial committee are holding flags with the 150th anniversary decal, which featured the colors of blue, green, red, and yellow.

Six

ANSWERING THE CALL

MILITARY

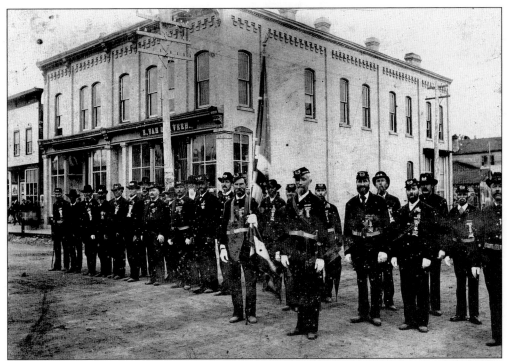

Civil War veterans, members of the A.C. Van Raalte Post #262, Grand Army of the Republic, converge at the corner of Eighth Street and River Avenue to prepare for a patriotic observance. Most of the veterans served in Company I, 25th Michigan Volunteer Infantry. They were mustered on August 14, 1862 and served, if able, until June 24, 1865. The Holland GAR post was organized July 17, 1884. Holland held its first Decoration Day in 1875 and the veterans were called the "Holland Soldiers' Association." Civil War veterans marched in every patriotic celebration including those held on the Fourth of July and Decoration Day, later called Memorial Day.

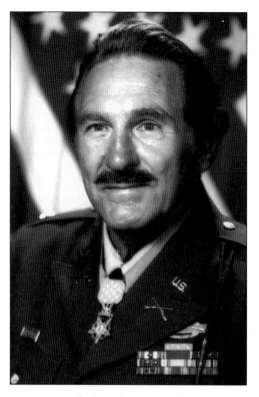

Almost 36 years from the day Lt. Col. Matt Urban checked out of an English hospital to rejoin his men at the Normandy, France fighting front, President Jimmy Carter draped the Congressional Medal of Honor around Urban's neck. The president made the presentation in Washington, D.C., on July 19, 1960. The supreme tribute to valor made Urban the most combat-decorated soldier in World War II. He had 29 other combat medals and medals of valor from France and Belgium. Seven times wounded, Urban spent 20 months in front-line action in six major battle campaigns in Algeria, Tunisia, Sicily, France, and Belgium. While convalescing from wounds, he heard about his unit's losses in France. He voluntarily left the hospital, hitch-hiked to the front at St. Lo and retook command of his company. Urban came to Holland in 1974 as City Recreation and Civic Center Director. In September 1980, the street leading to the DAV hall and West 49th Street was named Matt Urban Drive. He retired in 1989 and died March 4, 1995 at the age of 75, and is buried in Arlington National Cemetery. His Medal of Honor citation concludes: "Captain Urban's personal leadership, limitless bravery and repeated extraordinary exposure to enemy fire served as an inspiration to his entire battalion."

On April 25, 1951, Cpl. John Essebagger sacrificed his life in a heroic one-man stand on a Korean battlefield, and posthumously received the Congressional Medal of Honor. The 22-year-old Essebagger was credited with single-handedly inflicting heavy losses on the enemy and disrupting their advance before he fell mortally wounded near Popsudong, Korea. Essebagger walked into murderous gunfire to stall an attack by Communist troops and permitted his buddies to withdraw to comparative safety. His company commander said the young hero accounted for an estimated 14 enemies killed and an untold number of wounded. Essebagger was a 1946 Holland High School graduate. He has a parade field named in his honor at Fort Benning, Georgia. He is buried in Pilgrim Home Cemetery. His Medal of Honor citation concludes: "His valorous conduct and devotion to duty reflected lasting glory upon himself and was in keeping with the noblest traditions of the infantry and the U.S. Army."

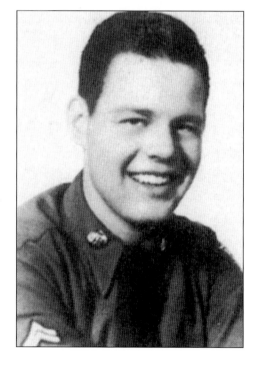

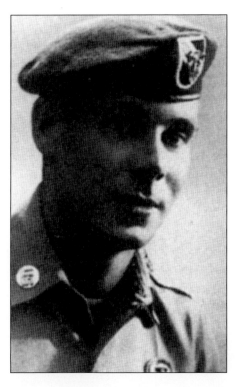

On January 18, 1968, Sgt. Gordon Yntema, who attended Holland High School and enlisted in the Army July 10, 1963, fell while engaged in a desperate fight with the Viet Cong in Thong Binh, Vietnam. For his heroic actions and courageous stand, Yntema was posthumously awarded the Congressional Medal of Honor. Outnumbered, wounded, and ordered to withdraw, Yntema refused to leave his comrades. He carried a wounded Vietnamese commander and a fatally wounded American Special Forces advisor to a gully to protect them from enemy fire. Out of ammunition, Yntema used his rifle as a club. Before he fell, Yntema had struck 15 Viet Cong who tried to capture him. A noncommissioned officer's club at Fort Bragg, North Carolina and the Holland AMVETS Post 1983 are named in his honor. His Medal of Honor citation concludes: "Sergeant Yntema's personal bravery in the face of insurmountable odds and supreme self-sacrifice were in keeping with the highest traditions of the military service and reflect the utmost credit upon himself, the 1st Special Forces and the U.S. Army."

Staff Sgt. Paul Lambers, a 1960 Holland Christian High School graduate, received the Congressional Medal of Honor on November 24, 1969 from President Richard Nixon in a White House East Room ceremony while his mother Jeannette Lambers looked on. Lambers' unit was attacked by a Viet Cong battalion on the night of August 20, 1968. He single-handedly repulsed penetration by detonating claymore mines and throwing well-aimed grenades, killing nine Viet Cong before the offensive was thwarted. Leaving his covered position, the 27-year-old crossed the fire-swept position to the recoilless rifle. Moving from position to position during the five-hour battle, Lambers repeatedly directed artillery and helicopter fire. He distributed ammunition and cared for wounded comrades, moving them to sheltered positions. On December 1, 1970, Lambers was swept away by high waves from the south breakwater at Holland Harbor. His body was never recovered. His Medal of Honor citation concludes: "Lambers' superb leadership, professional skill and magnificent courage saved the lives of his comrades, resulted in the virtual annihilation of a vastly superior enemy force and was largely instrumental in thwarting an enemy offensive against Tay Ninh City, Vietnam."

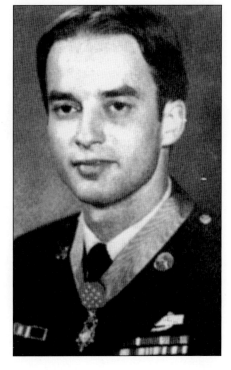

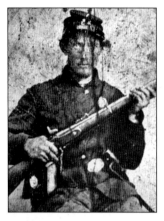

Pvt. Johannes Van Lente of Holland served in Company I, 25th Infantry Regiment. Van Lente enlisted at age 27 in 1862. In addition to fighting at the battle of Tebbs Bend, Kentucky, July 4, 1863, he participated in several battles. While advancing on Atlanta in General Sherman's March to the Sea on May 14, 1864, Van Lente was involved in fighting around Resaca, Georgia. During the fighting, he witnessed the death of his good friend Cornelius Van Dam. He lost his knapsack and all of his belongings: paper, money, pens, sewing equipment, a Bible, photographs, food, and grooming items. Van Lente contracted pneumonia and was taken to a hospital in Altoona, Georgia. He was later transferred to Marietta, Georgia where he remained until November 1864. While convalescing, Van Lente worked as a cook.

Pvt. Pieter Ver Schure (left) was Holland's only fatality in the Tebbs Bend battle. He and Jan Albers (right) were members of Company I, 25th Regiment. Ver Schure was killed fighting against Confederate General John Hunt Morgan's unit. He is interred in the National Cemetery in Lebanon, Kentucky.

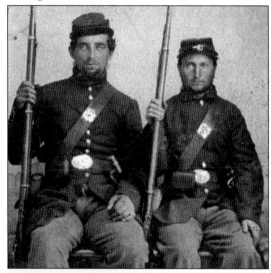

Civil War veterans are marching in a Memorial Day parade on River Avenue adjacent to Centennial Park in 1912. A young fisherman (right) accompanies the men. The Grand Army of the Republic (GAR) stone was placed in the park on October 9, 1912.

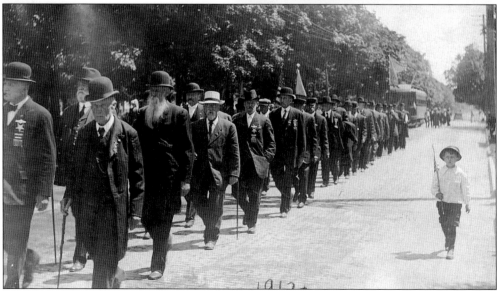

82

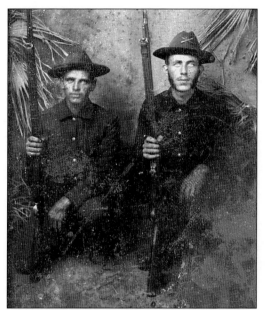

Pvt. Martinus (Tien) Vande Water (right) and his Holland friend served in Company E of the 32nd Regiment during the Spanish-American War. Vande Water suffered from typhoid fever and returned to Holland in November 1898. Most of the unit arrived home on September 30, 1898 on a special railroad car to take part in a celebration featuring Michigan Governor Hazen Pingree.

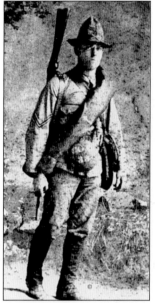

Pvt. Charles Hiler of Holland, who served in the 105-day Spanish-American War, wore his full battle gear posing at the E.J. O'Leary Studio. Hiler and his brother, Cpl. William Hiler, as members of the 33rd Regiment of the Michigan Infantry, participated in the battle of Santiago, Cuba July 1–17, 1898.

Four Holland men relax in front of their tent while stationed with the 32nd Regiment in Fort Clinch near Fernandina, Florida, in the summer of 1898. Most of the volunteers remained in Florida for training and did not see combat.

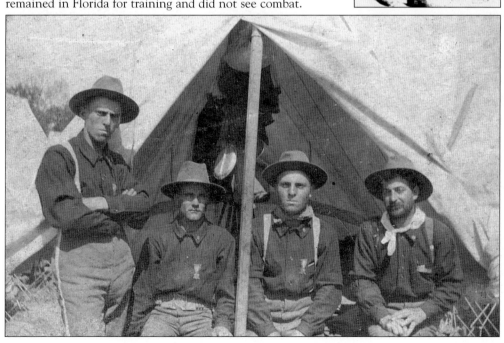

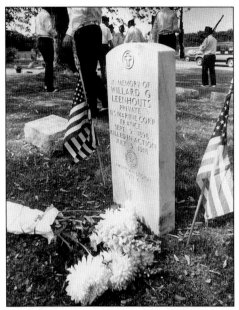

Pvt. Willard Leenhouts, 19, was Holland's first soldier killed in World War I. He was at Belleau Woods Hill, France, and was killed by shrapnel on July 3, 1918. Although the War Department telegram indicated the body was to be returned to the United States at the war's end, Leenhouts' body was permanently interred in France. His parents, Dr. and Mrs. Abraham Leenhouts, visited the Aisene Marne Cemetery at Belleau Woods in 1930. In 1919, Holland veterans named their American Legion unit Willard G. Leenhouts Post. Post 6 members erected a memorial monument in 1992 in Pilgrim Home Cemetery honoring Leenhouts.

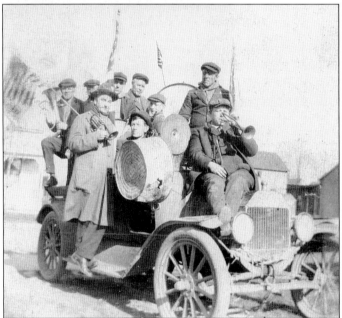

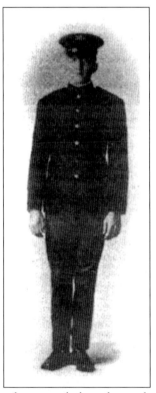

Left: The Holland City Gas Co. Brass Band, featuring horns, bass drum, symbols and a wash tub, celebrated Armistice Day, November 11, 1918. The celebration marked the end of World War I. Parading began at 7 a.m. and featured decorated automobiles, trucks, and bands. A huge bonfire at River Avenue and 15th Street concluded the day after the parade ended at 6 p.m.

Right: Pvt. Henry Walters was Holland's second man to die in World War I. The Holland Veterans of Foreign Wars Post 2144 is named in his honor. Walters died July 15, 1918 of wounds received during the battle of Chateau-Thierry, France. Walters' body was returned to the United States and services were held August 1, 1921. He was buried in Pilgrim Home Cemetery. The VFW Post was founded in 1931.

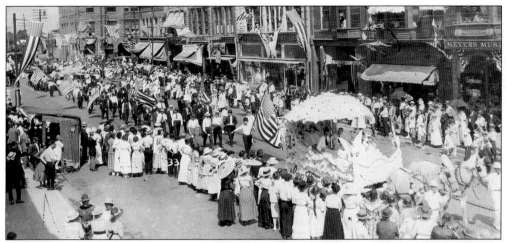

Holland residents filled the street and sidewalk on Eighth Street in 1919 to celebrate the first Fourth of July after the end of World War I.

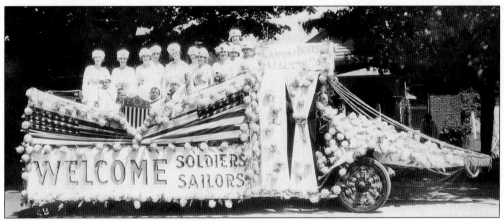

Women from the Cappon-Bertsch Leather Company, flanked by children, wear red crosses on their caps. They are on a float to welcome Holland soldiers and sailors July 4, 1919.

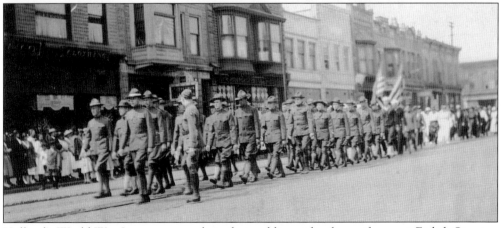

Holland's World War I veterans march in their soldier and sailor uniforms on Eighth Street.

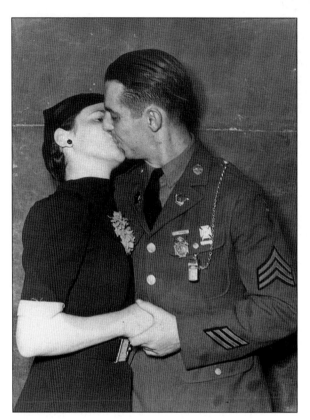

This wedding kiss was in newspapers worldwide following a ceremony January 15, 1937, while Holland National Guards were on sit-down strike duty in Flint, Michigan at Fisher Body plants. Sgt. Arthur Woltman of Holland had planned to be married January 15 to Miss Frances Annesley of Saugatuck. Woltman was not permitted to leave Flint. He called his bride and she drove, along with her sister and brother-in-law to Flint where the couple was married in a school assembly hall. The nuptials were witnessed by the entire First Battalion in full dress uniform, including Holland's Company D. Congratulated by the regiment, the couple kissed for *Flint Journal* photographer G.V. Smith. The picture circulated in newspapers throughout the United States and the rest of the world, including one from Cairo, Egypt. The clippings are in Mrs. Woltman's scrapbook. Sgt. Woltman died in 1991 at the age of 79, and his widow died in 2002 at 86.

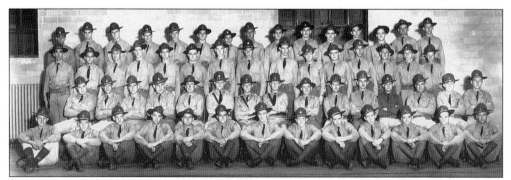

Company D of the 126th Infantry of the Holland National Guard spent 36 days on strike duty, from January 12 to February 16, 1937, at the General Motors automobile plant in Flint, Michigan. More than 1,500 Michigan guardsmen were mobilized after 18 people were injured in rioting. The strike was resolved, without firing a shot, and workers returned to their jobs. The Holland unit was given an appreciation dinner by the Holland Chamber of Commerce in the Warm Friend Tavern. They were photographed in the Holland Armory.

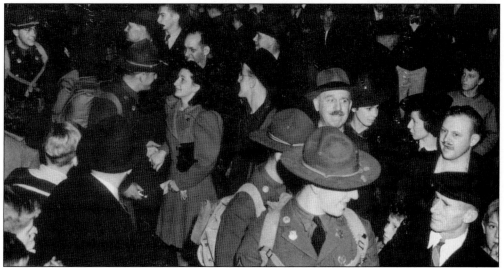

This is part of the crowd of 5,000 people who gathered at the Holland Pere Marquette train depot on October 25, 1940 to bid farewell to Holland's Company D of the126th Infantry. The troops left for Camp Beauregard, Louisiana, at 10:15 p.m. The troops had marched from the Holland Armory on Eighth Street to the depot. Citizens lined both sides of the street. Several marched along the street beside the guardsmen. Saying good-byes are Cpl. Clarence (Babe) Kuhlman (center) and Wanda Stranisz, the future Mrs. Kuhlman. At far let is Pfc. Osborne Vos. Sgt. Homer Lokker is at right foreground. Company D was leaving Holland for a year's military training. Little did this unit of three officers and 77 enlisted men realize that the company flag would fly many places before the end of World War II. During this period the unit, as part of the 32nd Division, saw 654 days of combat. Of the original company, nine men were killed in action in the Southwest Pacific, one was killed in a military airplane accident, 11 were wounded in action, and many were ravaged by malaria, blackwater fever, tropical ulcers, high temperatures, and malnutrition.

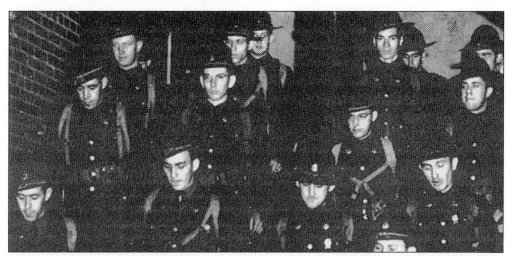

Members of Company D walk down the Holland Armory steps en route to the Pere Marquette depot and a special train. Two of the men pictured, Pfc. Paul Henagin and Pvt. Robert John, were killed fighting. Henagin died November 27, 1942 in New Guinea and was Holland's first victim of the war in the Pacific. John was killed April 16, 1944 in Arawe, New Britain.

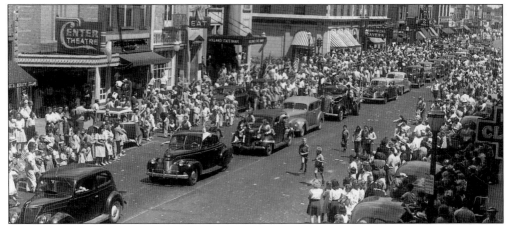

Crowds and cars congregate on Eighth Street on August 15, 1945 to celebrate the victory over Japan, V-J Day, the end of World War II.

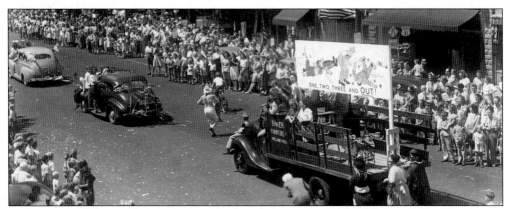

A Baker Furniture truck carries a large sign: "One, Two Three and Out!" as part of the V-J Day parade. Drawn by Baker employee and artist Ed Brolin, the characters show Uncle Sam flexing his muscles while Axis powers' representatives are "knocked out."

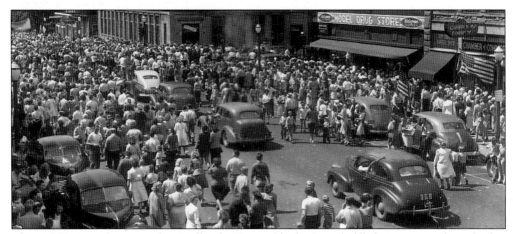

The V-J Day parade approaches Holland's Tower Clock. Crowds fill the streets as the vehicles, all built before 1942, head to the parade's end at Kollen Park.

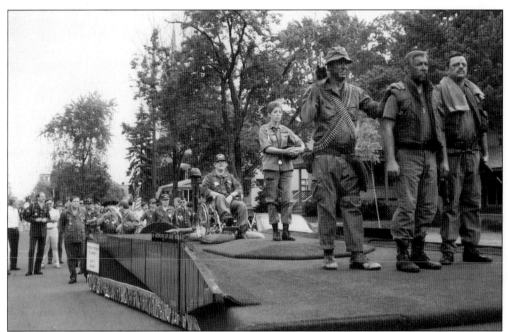

With the names of the 2,648 Michigan people who died in the Vietnam War listed on the float's side, Holland Chapter 73 of the Vietnam Veterans of America appeared first in the 1989 tulip festival. The three soldiers in front represented the fighting combat infantry, depicting the three-man statue next to the Vietnam War Memorial in Washington, D.C. Behind is a nurse, who cared for the wounded, represented by Pfc. Carl Poest, followed by a field cross. The cross is composed of an upside down M-16 weapon with bayonet, plunged into the ground, and topped with a helmet on top. "Dog tags" (identification) are draped on the weapon.

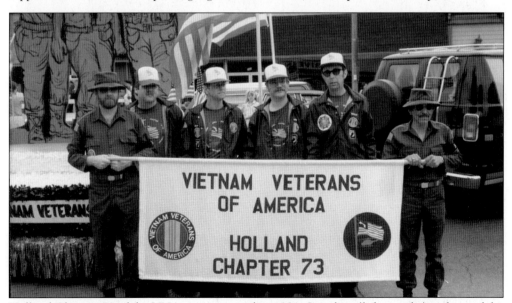

Holland Chapter 73 of the VVA was organized in 1981. Standing (left to right) in front of the Tulip Time float are: Don Inman, Craig De Feyter, Bob Hieftje, Carl Poest, "Hondo" Robinson and Ed Garcia.

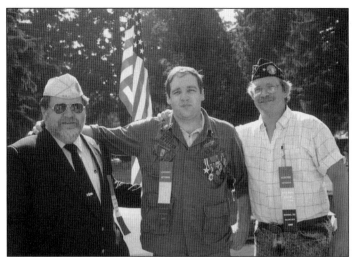

Three members of the Holland chapter of the VVA participated in the 1991 Memorial Day parade and services. They are as follows: (left to right) Rich Straub, Craig De Feyter, and Carl Poest.

The 1985 VVA color guard in 1985 was composed of Bob Taylor, Don Inman, Jesus (Jessie) Sanabria, Jack Esenhaur, Ken Hollar, Ed Garcia, and Steve Chapman.

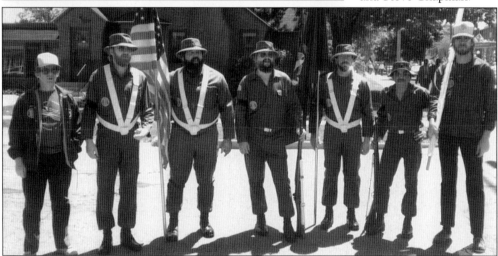

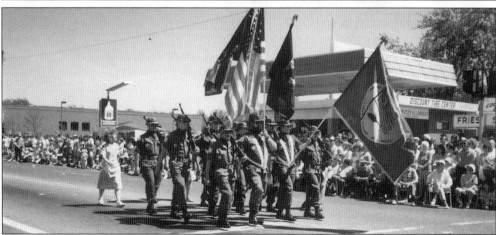

The VVA honor guard, followed by two nurses, marched in Holland and western Michigan festival parades. Vietnam veterans have participated in Tulip Time and Memorial Day parades since 1975.

Holland men and women responded to the Desert Storm military action in 1991. Residents, including Jennifer Bushre, signed a "Thank You and Welcome Home" card in front of the Holland Post Office.

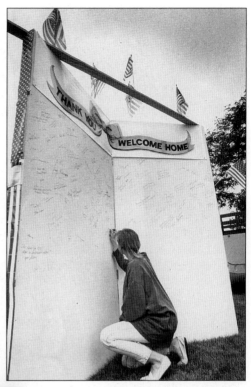

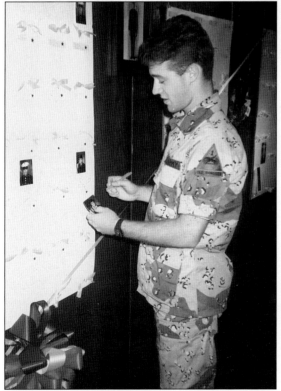

When Scott Poest served in Desert Storm, it marked the third generation of Poests who had served in military combat. Upon his return, Scott was honored in the VFW Hall where he removed his picture and yellow ribbon from the picture-ribbon board of Desert Storm military personnel. He then attached the ribbon to his uniform. Scott's father, Carl, was wounded in Vietnam and Scott's grandfather served in combat during World War II. The Poests are natives of Zeeland, Michigan, located five miles east of Holland.

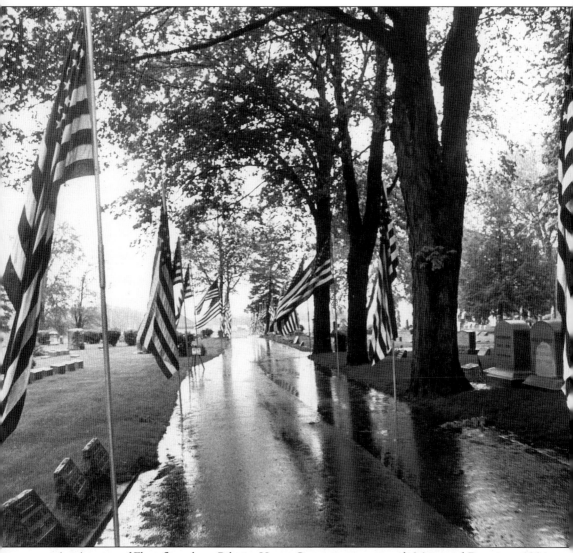

An Avenue of Flags flies along Pilgrim Home Cemetery streets each Memorial Day since 1984. Placed by veterans' organizations, casket flags were donated by more than 350 families of deceased Holland veterans.

Seven

RESPLENDENT RESORTS

TOURISM

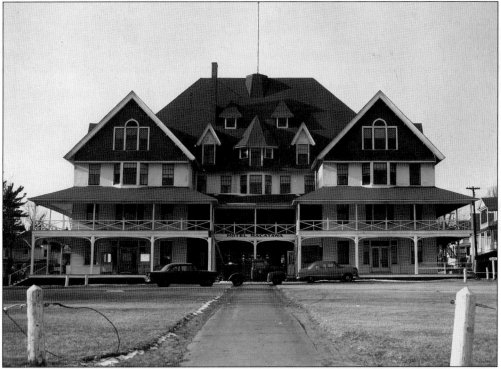

Opened in 1895, the Macatawa Hotel stood at the west end of Lake Macatawa and welcomed summer visitors through 1955. Torn down in 1956 because of the high operational costs and necessary structural alterations, the hotel had served 13,000 guests in 115 rooms the previous year. Included in the hotel complex were stores, a post office, a pavilion, and an inclined cog railway that carried spectators to the top of a sand dune overlooking Lake Michigan. Cottages were located around the hotel.

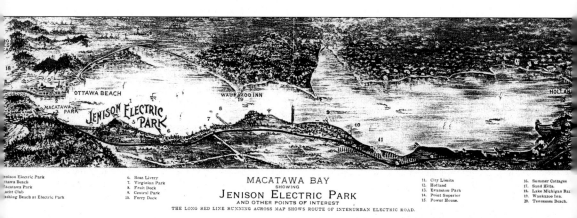

MACATAWA BAY

SHOWING

JENISON ELECTRIC PARK

AND OTHER POINTS OF INTEREST

THE LONG RED LINE RUNNING ACROSS MAP SHOWS ROUTE OF INTERURBAN ELECTRIC ROAD.

Jenison Electric Park
Ottawa Beach
Macatawa Park
Yacht Club
Bathing Beach at Electric Park

6. Boat Livery
7. Virginian Park
8. Fruit Dock
9. Central Park
10. Ferry Dock

11. City Limits
12. Holland
13. Evanston Park
14. Point Superior
15. Power House.

16. Summer Cottages
17. Sand Hills.
18. Lake Michigan Bath
19. Waukazoo Inn.
20. Tennessee Beach.

This drawing of Macatawa Bay, showing Jenison Electric Park in 1903, noted all of the resorts on the south and north sides of Lake Macatawa and Ottawa Beach on Lake Michigan.

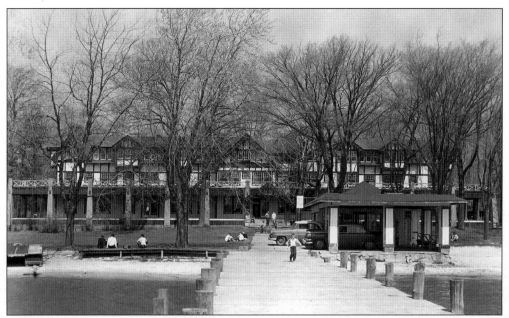

Waukazoo Inn was built in 1902, and was enlarged to house 75 rooms for 200 guests in 1909. Chicago judge John Everett and Holland attorney John Post purchased the property from Hope College for $25,000 in 1901. Plans for Hope to develop a Hope Haven University featuring a School of Science never materialized. The inn was located on Indian Point on the north side of Lake Macatawa at the foot of the Waukazoo woods. Cottages were built adjacent to and near the inn. The inn was razed in 1960. Native Americans had lived in the area in the early 1800s, leaving in 1849 after the Dutch settlement of Holland was established about six miles away.

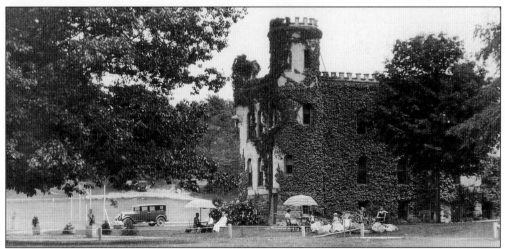

Castle Park, located a few miles south of Lake Macatawa and several hundred yards from Lake Michigan, opened as a resort in 1896. The castle was built as a home in the 1880s by Michael Schwarz, a Chicago realtor who had fled to the United States during the Franco-Prussian war. His family didn't like the isolation and a Chicago minister found the abandoned castle while chaperoning a group of students in 1893. He bought the property for a summer camp. His nephew Carter Brown bought the resort in 1917 and planted the ivy. Cottages are built around the castle grounds. The castle is now used for wedding receptions and private parties.

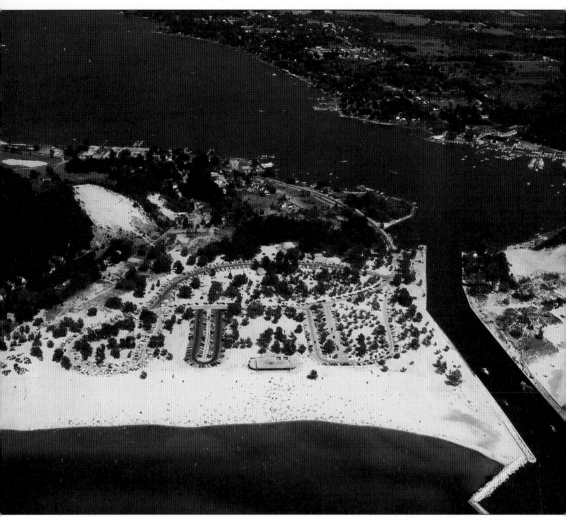

Holland State Park at Ottawa Beach officially opened in the summer of 1928. Three years earlier, the Michigan Park Board accepted a county proposal for a state park. The first 18 acres were increased to 32 acres in 1927. People began using this sandy beach in 1858 and it was called Ottawa Beach. This photo was taken 40 years ago. In 1964, the Michigan Conservation Commission purchased 90 acres (center, behind trees), formerly Ottawa Beach golf course, for additional campgrounds. The land was bought from Mr. and Mrs. Martin Michielsen for $127,000. Mount Pisgah, the highest dune, is at the left. The state park annually leads Michigan in attendance with 1.7 million visitors.

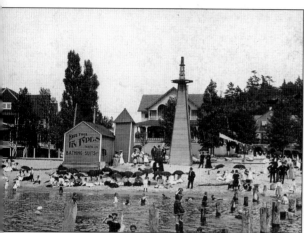

"Have your Tin Types taken in bathing suits," was advertised a century ago for Macatawa Park bathers on Lake Michigan's shore.

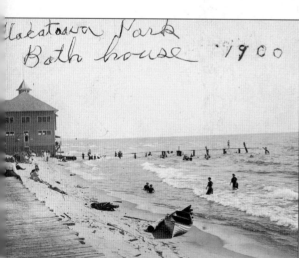

Macatawa Park
Bath house "1900

As the 20th Century arrived, bathers frolicked in Lake Michigan and used the Macatawa Park bath house.

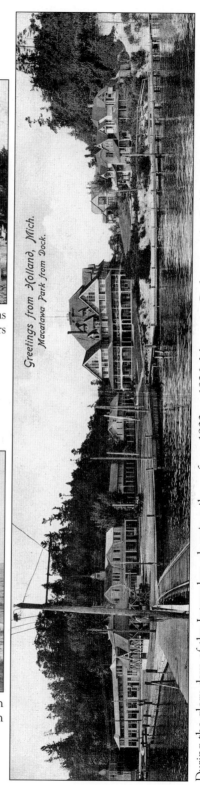

Greetings from Holland, Mich.
Macatawa Park from Dock.

During the glory days of the Interurban electric railway, from 1900 to 1926, Macatawa Park enjoyed a heyday. This post card was published about 90 years ago.

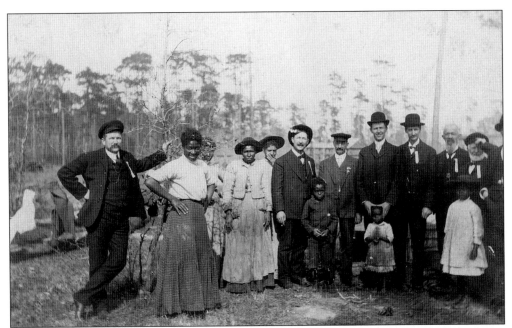

Pictured here are Interurban riders in the early 1900s. They are most likely railway employees, family members of hotel and cottage workers, and resorters who worked or resorted at Jenison Park or Macatawa Park.

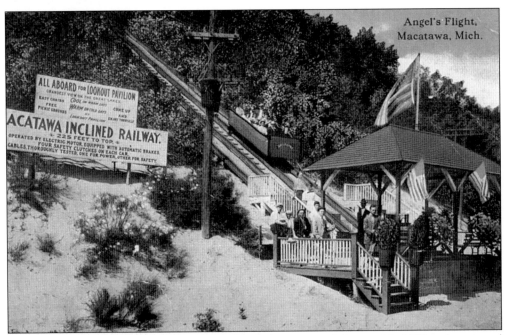

Angel's Flight, a cog railway up a Macatawa Park dune, opened August 14, 1909 and prospered for 13 years. Two cable cars were electrically controlled from the park's pavilion. The inclined railway was 190 feet long with two cable cars, one descending and the other ascending. They ran on a 45-degree slope between the waiting station at the top and the pavilion. It was advertised to be 225 feet to the top.

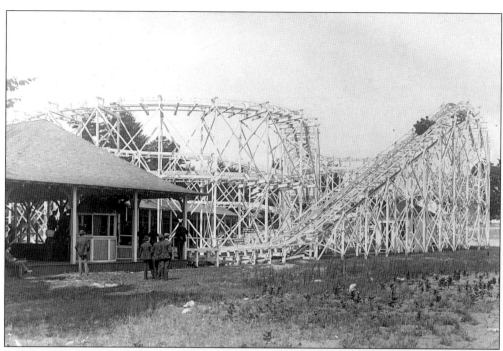

Roller coaster rides made Jenison Electric Park an exciting amusement place. Opened in 1892, the amusement park was made electric in 1903. The roller coaster was a popular attraction, opening in 1908. The park continued until the demise of the Interurban electric railway in 1926.

A balloon flight was a weekly attraction at Jenison Park and other sites around Holland early in the 20th Century. Featuring a specially attired entertainer, the flights drew crowds at summer factory and farmer picnics. They were always a feature attraction at "Venetian Nights" when all types of watercraft paraded in Lake Macatawa.

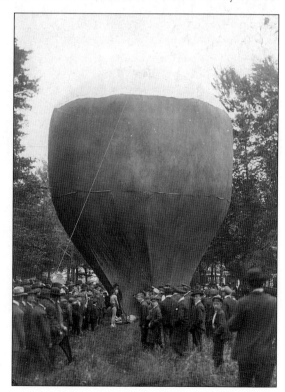

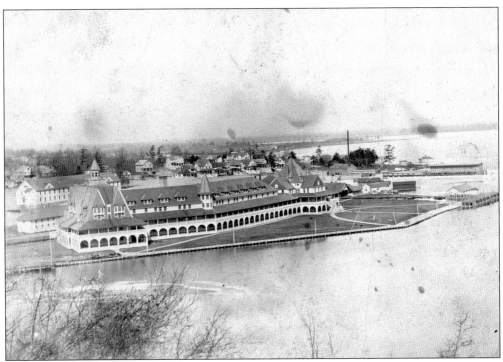

First constructed in 1886 and enlarged in 1901, the spacious Ottawa Beach Hotel sat on the north side of Lake Macatawa along the bend of the channel. The top of the hotel was 152 feet long and featured 185 rooms with dining facilities for 535 people. Cottages were located behind the facility. The hotel was destroyed by fire on November 6, 1923, just following a $15,000 addition. Defective wiring had caused the blaze, and it was never rebuilt.

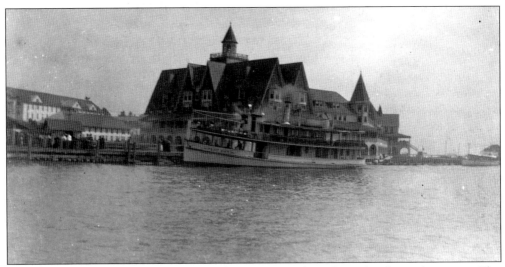

Ferry boats transported resorters across Lake Macatawa throughout the day and evening. This excursion boat *Post Boy* is unloading passengers at the Ottawa Beach Hotel during the 20th Century's first decade. The hotel, with its complex in the background, was located on Ottawa Beach Road, just east of Ottawa Beach. Owned by the Pere Marquette Railway, the hotel had 398 feet of channel frontage. The veranda was designed by famed architect William Williamson.

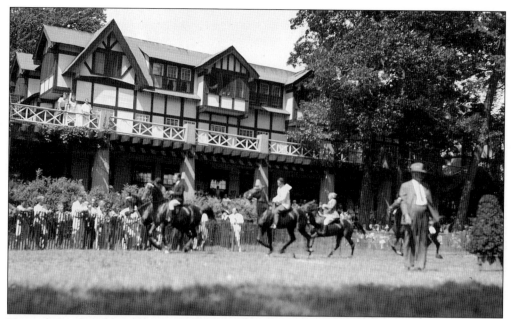

Horse shows, featuring three- and five-gaited horses in various competitions, including jumping fences, provided popular entertainment in front of the Waukazoo Inn. First staged in 1932, the event attracted several hundred spectators. Held on Saturday, the horse show began with a luncheon, followed by the horse event. Dinner followed and a dance concluded the day. On Sunday, a professional instrumentalist entertained in concert.

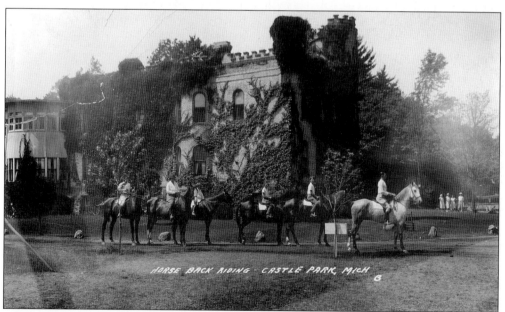

Billed as one of Michigan's oldest amateur horse shows, having started in 1922, the Castle Park event occurred on the last Wednesday in August. Because of the size of the grounds surrounding Castle Park, the most exciting event was "hunters over the outside course." Several of the barriers were natural, including stone elevations and bridges. Horse shows held at the Castle attracted equestrians from throughout the Midwest, as well as Olympic performers.

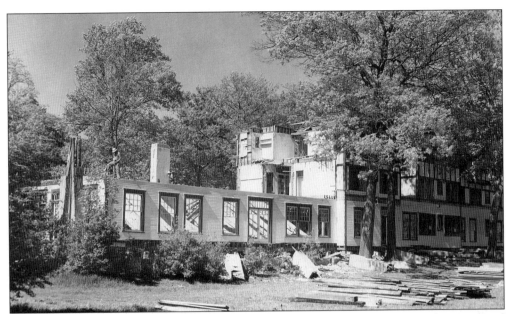

Razed in April 1960, the Waukazoo Inn was demolished because the unheated resort hotel could not compete with more modern facilities. Residential development in the Waukazoo woods started in 1957. Other residential developments followed with the reorganization of the Waukazoo Woods Association, founded in the 1920s.

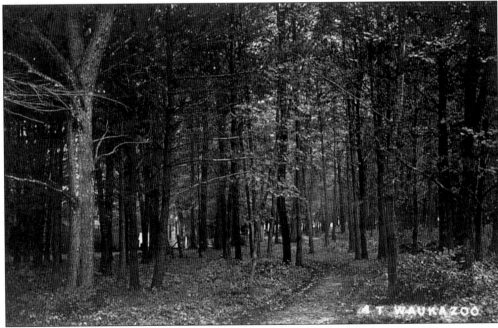

Before it became a popular place to develop new homes, the Waukazoo woods area was a densely populated section of forest on Holland's north side. A few bridal paths, for horseback riding and pedestrians, were the only way to travel north from the inn to the Ottawa Beach Road. Although still wooded, year-round homes occupy much of the area; it has become one of the Holland vicinity's most favorable residential locations.

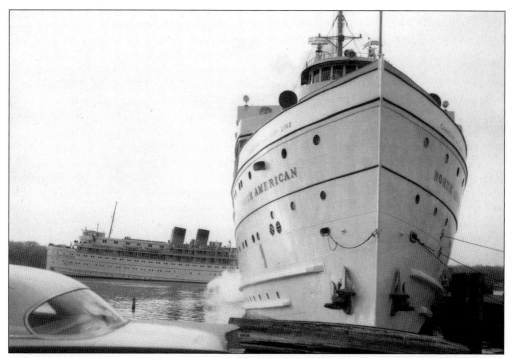

Beginning in 1914, summer passenger liners the *S.S. South American*, the *S.S. North American*, and, for several years, the *S.S. Alabama* (not pictured), moored at the Montello Park docks at the foot of West 16th Street during the winter months. Owned by the Chicago, Duluth, and Georgian Bay Transit Company, the ships plied the Great Lakes throughout the summer. They returned to Holland every September until 1958, when the ships were sold. The *North* sank off Nantucket Island in 1967, the *South* was dismantled in Baltimore in 1992, and the *Alabama* was converted into a crane barge, where it still operates in Saginaw Bay.

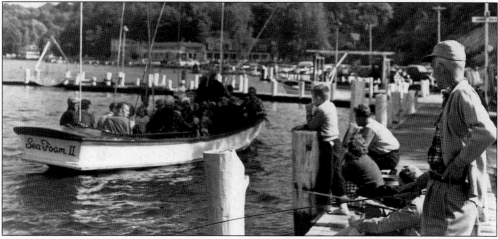

In the early 1920s, former Coast Guardsman Neal (Casey) Landman started a livery service to transport fishermen and women from the Macatawa Park dock to the north and south piers. Bamboo poles and long tree branches were popular with anglers. Landman provided his service from the mid-1920s until the mid-1950s and those fishing received parking privileges near the dock.

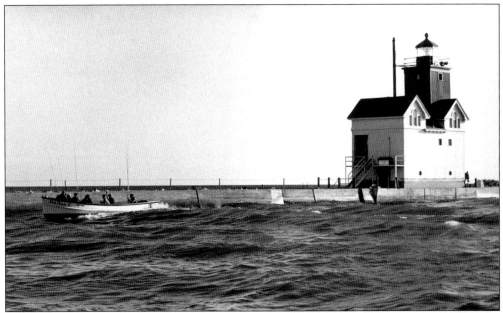

In 1956, before the U.S. Corps of Engineers hired Vern Bush of Holland to sandblast the lighthouse with special sand from Spring Lake, Michigan, the building had been yellow. The facility was repainted "navigation red" and acquired the name "Big Red." That color was the standard color for all lighthouses at the time, according to 1956 Holland Coast Guard station commander Walter Seals. The lighthouse has been inoperative for many years. Landman's fishing boat is at left after having picked up anglers from the south pier.

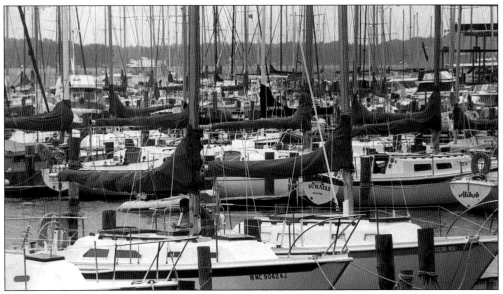

The forest of masts pictured here can be glimpsed every summer at the Lake Macatawa docking and slip sections. Photographed in 1984, today only the sizes and types of sailing and power craft have changed. Eldean's Shipyard and the Macatawa Bay Yacht Club are nearby. The Jesiek Brothers operated the first boat service on Lake Macatawa in 1911 and sold it to the Eldeans in 1973.

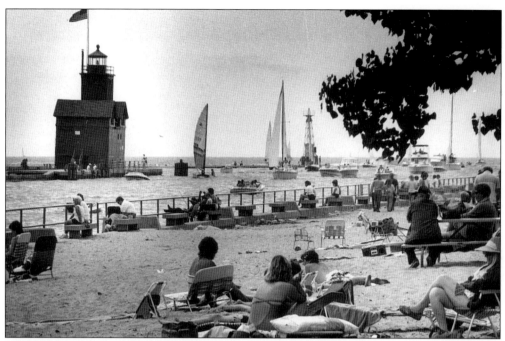

Holland State Park, with "Big Red" serving as a sentinel on the south breakwater, draws crowds to its sugar-sand beach. Relaxing, picnicking, or watching people, sailboats and power boats in the Holland Harbor channel are always good ways to wile away the time. Scenes like these seldom change, as witnessed in this 1986 Labor Day weekend picture.

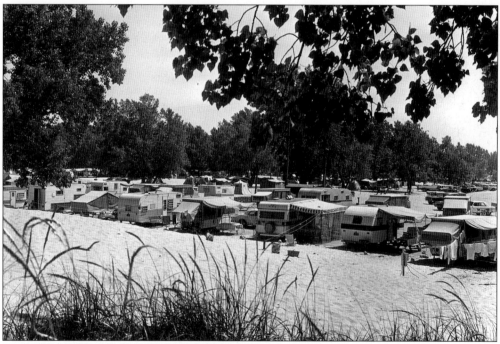

Trailers have filled Ottawa Beach every week for many years. This 1960s scene repeats itself annually at the state park and its annex, located at the park "oval."

MICHIGAN'S MOST SCENIC BOAT RIDE

ON THE WATERS OF

Lake Michigan and Lake Macatawa

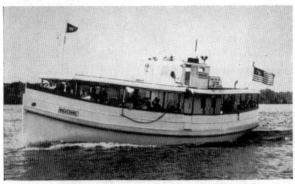

TWO HOUR CRUISE

ADULTS:

$1.00

CHILDREN: (Under 12)

60¢

Round Trip

Leaves Kollen Park Daily:

Main Dock at Foot of West 10th Street, Kollen Park, Holland, Michigan

1:00 P.M.
3:00 P.M.
5:00 P.M.
7:00 P.M.
9:00 P.M.

Thru Labor Day—Weather Permitting

THE FERRY BOAT **WOLVERINE** (HOLLAND)

SEVENTY PASSENGERS — GOVERNMENT INSPECTED — DIESEL POWERED

Docks at Kollen Park, Waukazoo Resort, Macatawa Hotel, Ottawa Beach Pier

A Treasure Trip for Camera Fans

You may take pictures of Large Lake Passenger Liners, Oil Tankers, Cement Carriers, Lake Freighters, Palatial Yachts, Beautiful Cabin Cruisers, also Sail Boat Races, Outbord Motor Races, Etc.

You may see Champion Skiers in Stunts, Thrills and Spills; Bathing Beauties and Expert Swimmers along the Shores and Beaches

Michigan Water Wonderland

- - - in all its Beauty

The WOLVERINE will take you along the wooded shores of Lake Macatawa and the white sandy shores of Lake Michigan, also the great and picturesque sand dunes. You will see many nice homes and fine estates, resort hotels and motels, summer cottages and cabins. You will cruise thru the Government Million Dollar Concrete Channel and Breakwater, past the Coast Guard Station, Lighthouse Towers and into the blue waters of Lake Michigan and along shores of Macatawa Resort and Ottawa Beach, one of Michigan's largest Trailer parks and Tented City, out into Lake Michigan, then back to Kollen Park, completing two hours of comfortable relaxing pleasure. Soft Drinks and Refreshments on the boat.

CHARTER PARTIES FOR CHURCHES, SCHOOLS & CLUBS

No Reservation Necessary for Small Groups. Step Aboard, No Ticket Needed

For Further Information See Capt. Ernest Wingard at Boat, Phone EX 2-3385, or Write 244 W. Ninth St.

THE FERRY BOAT **WOLVERINE** (HOLLAND)

Member Holland Chamber of Commerce & Western Michigan Tourist Association

Main Dock at Foot of West Tenth Street, Kollen Park, Holland, Michigan

FREE PARKING AND PICNICKING PRIVILEGES IN KOLLEN PARK

The ferry boat *Wolverine* operated a passenger service from the 1940s through the 1960s. Similar boat services started as long ago as the 1880s.

Eight

TULIP TIME TOWN FESTIVAL

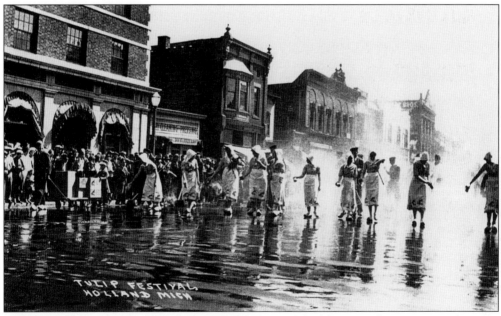

Experiments in scrubbing streets with "Dutch Cleanser" had been tried just prior to the 1931 Tulip Time Festival. In an advance publicity stunt to promote the festival, two blocks of Eighth Street, between River and College Avenues, were scrubbed with Dutch Cleanser. Following the city water wagon were ten Holland High School girls, dressed in "Little Dutch Cleanser" costumes and wooden shoes. Scrubbers were businessmen carrying wide brooms which they used to scrub the cobblestone street. The entire process took 45 minutes, while Fox and Universal News Reel shot movies and recorded the sounds of the babble on the streets for use in theaters throughout the country. Traffic was suspended during the production. Because of the residue left on the pavement, the stunt was never tried again. But the nation's theatergoers witnessed Tulip Time street scrubbing in Holland, Michigan, a tradition that has continued for 73 years.

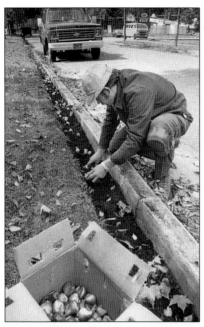

Holland city park department employees plant 203,000 new tulip bulbs every fall. Several varieties are planted and are divided into early, middle and later blossoming sections. Tulips are purchased from bulb growers in the Netherlands and arrive in crates. Holland has eight miles of tulip lanes and more than 750,000 tulips. With hundreds of homes and businesses growing tulips, the community boasts about six million blooms, which delight festival visitors for two weeks every May. The festival's slogan: "It's Tulip Time in Holland, Every Year in May."

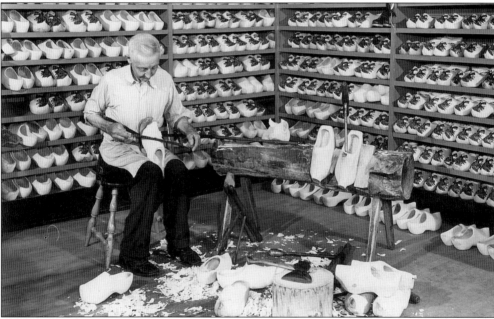

Gerrit Ten Brink was a wooden shoe carver at the Dutch Novelty Shop in the 1930s and 1940s. Ten Brink, 85 years old in 1943 and a native of the Netherlands, said he once finished 19 pairs of shoes in one day. During World War II, Ten Brink produced seven or eight pairs a day by hand, because "klompen" (Dutch for wooden shoes) makers were flooded with orders from war plants, acid manufacturers, and numerous other firms. Some orders were for farmers who wore wooden shoes in the fields. Every pair was accompanied by a reminder that wooden shoes do not bend like leather footwear and extra heavy socks were needed. Ten Brink's shoes outfitted hundreds of high school Dutch Dancers. He also made shoes for celebrities who attended the festival. Painters did the decorating and names were burned into the wood.

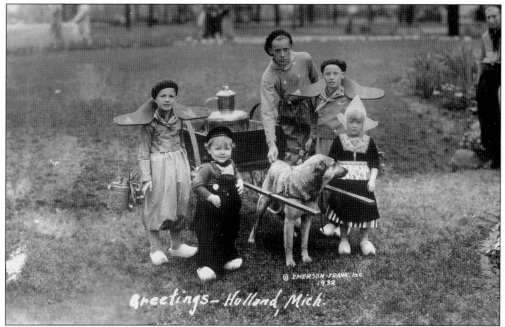

Lindy gained nationwide fame as the dog that pulled the Dutch milk cart, from the first Tulip Time parades through 1937. Owned by the Harry White family of Route 3, Holland, Lindy was ten years old when struck by a car and killed on June 15, 1937. He was purchased for nine-year-old Roy White and named after Charles A. Lindbergh, who had completed his historic New York-Paris solo non-stop flight in 1927.

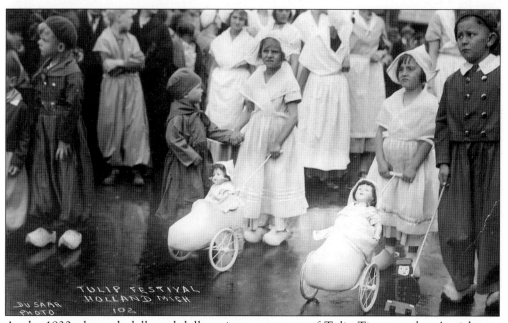

As the 1930s dawned, dolls and doll carriages were part of Tulip Time parades. At right are Janet and Jimmy Brooks, of the Phillips Brooks family of Holland. The elder Brooks was the founder of the Seven-Up Bottling Co. of Western Michigan.

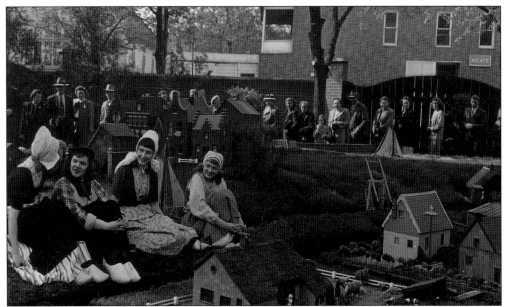

Little Netherlands became a part of Tulip Time in 1938. All of the buildings, people and animals were carved by hand. Visitors flocked to the miniature Dutch village located behind the Netherlands Museum on the northeast corner of Thirteenth Street and Central Avenue. This photograph was taken a decade later and shows Holland High School Dutch Dancers chatting. They are Arlene Beekman, Gwen Kooiker, Dorothy Brower, and Doris Harringsma.

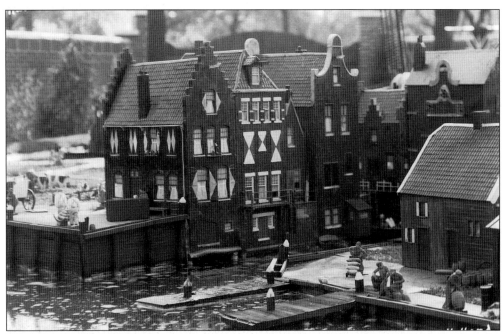

This close-up of the Little Netherlands shows the Dutch architecture of the homes and the figures busy preparing materials to be shipped on the canals. When Windmill Island opened in 1965, the Little Netherlands was moved to a building on the island. Here tourists enjoy a replica of urban and rural life in the Netherlands generations ago.

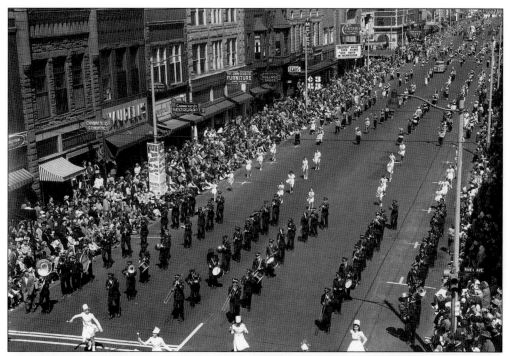

The Holland High School band, preceded by a drum major and majorettes, marches in the Children's Parade in 1951. Following are twirlers and Dutch-costumed youngsters. A Kiltie Band Concert at Riverview Park was a festival feature, according to a sign outside the festival headquarters in the Chamber of Commerce. Moviegoers were enjoying *Quo Vadis* in Technicolor.

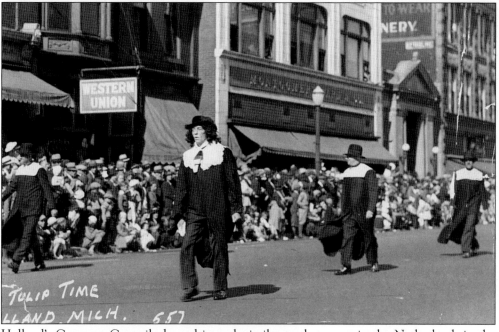

Holland's Common Council, dressed in garb similar to that worn in the Netherlands in the 19th Century, walked in the Volks (Folks) Parade during the festival's first few years.

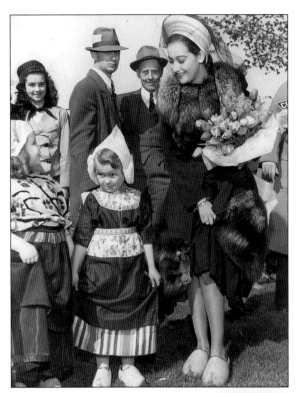

Glamorous motion picture star Dorothy Lamour visited Tulip Time's opening day in 1940. William H. Vande Water, *Grand Rapids Press* correspondent, is in the background along with Dutch Dancer Joanne van der Velde. The little girls, Mary Lou Van Dyke and Mary Lou Buis, presented the actress with a bouquet of tulips. Brought to Holland by the Holland Furnace Company, movie stars arrived by plane or on the train in a special car. The stars, including radio personalities and orchestra leaders, came from 1938 through 1941. They participated in a national radio show broadcast from Holland and included Virginia Grey, Rochelle Hudson, Robert Cummings, Richard Arlen, George Raft, Fay Wray, Simone Simon, and Pat O'Brien. The *National Barn Dance* and the *Professor Quiz* national radio shows were also broadcast from Holland during the festival.

A gift from the people of Amsterdam in 1947, this barrel organ was a popular entry in the succeeding festival parades and provided a fine ride for Dutch Dancers. Because the Amsterdam residents were grateful for the financial help and clothing provided by Holland, Michigan residents during World War II, they reciprocated during the community's Centennial year. The organ, refurbished in 1996, is on Windmill Island and is part of the annual festival parades.

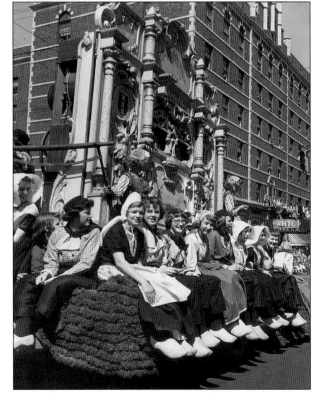

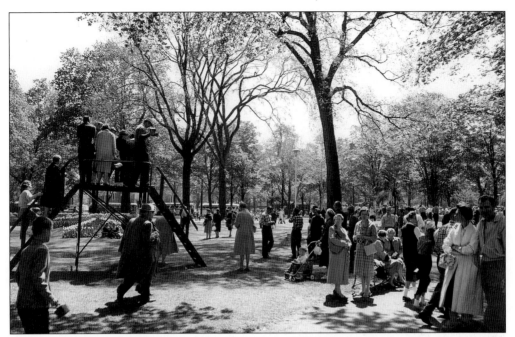

Taking advantage of an elevated photographic spot, Tulip Time visitors visually recorded the tulips and "mill" around in Centennial Park. The windmill bed of tulips is a favorite. These tourists, with their buses in the background, toured the festival about 40 years ago.

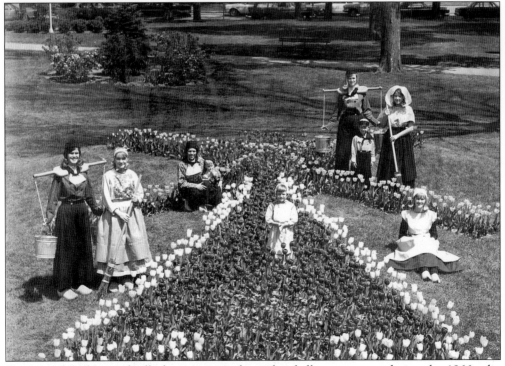

Centennial Park's windmill planting invited people of all ages to pose during the 1966 tulip festival.

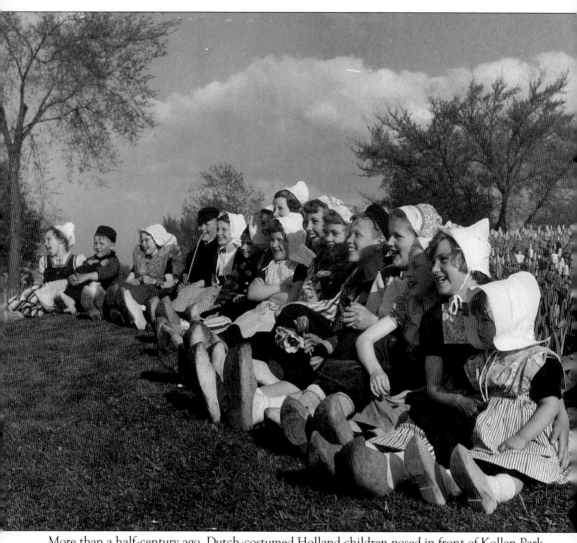

More than a half-century ago, Dutch-costumed Holland children posed in front of Kollen Park tulips.

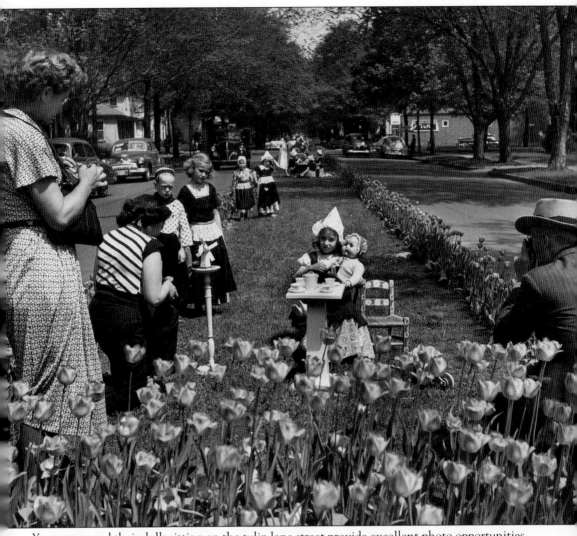

Youngsters and their dolls sitting on the tulip lane street provide excellent photo opportunities.

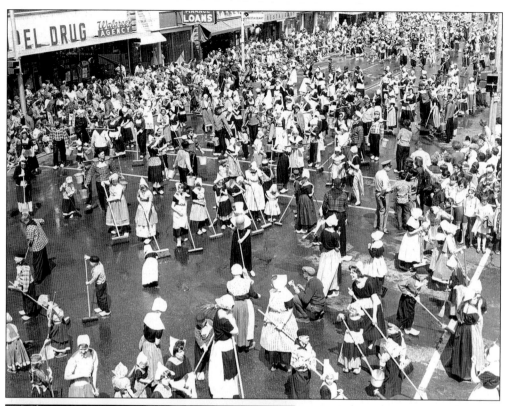

Street scrubbers, a tradition epitomizing Dutch cleanliness, fill the parade route prior to every year's Tulip Time Volks Parade.

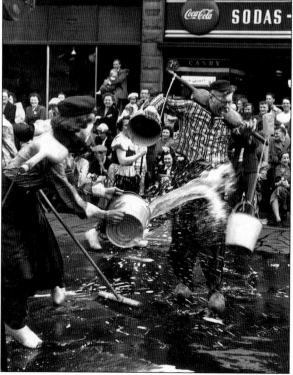

When May weather is warm, throwing water becomes a part of the street scrubbing.

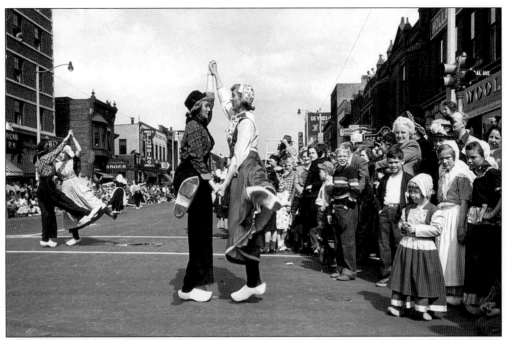

At least 30 times during the festival, the world famous Dutch Dance is performed by more than 1,200 high school girls, a few boys, and graduates.

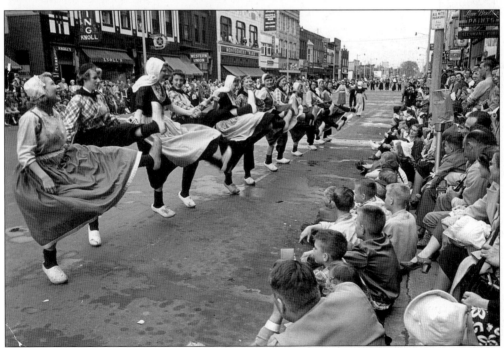

Lots of laughter accompanies these Dutch Dancers in 1950 as they perform some high kicks on Holland's scrubbed street. Pictured from left to right are the following: Judy Kronemeyer, Donna Tanis, Virginia Koning, Karel-Mari Kleinheksel, De Lene Barr, Anne Beerboom, Jeanne Cook, Myra Saunders, Marianne De Weese, Joan Souter, Jean De Pree, and Gloria Bear.

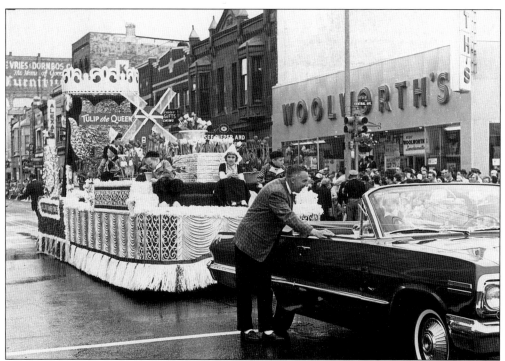

"Tulip the Queen" is the annual statement made at Tulip Time; it was inscribed on part of the Chamber of Commerce float more than 30 years ago. Since the festival's first year, Tulip Time officials emphasized that the tulip would be queen.

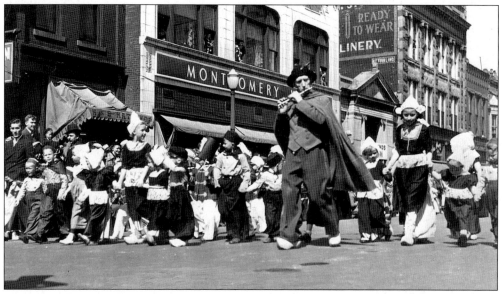

From 1937 through 1939, Neal Dalman, the Warm Friend Tavern elevator operator, played the role of Tulip Time's Pied Piper. While Dalman played his fife, Holland pre-school children paraded, joined by sisters, brothers, or friends under ten years old. Dalman's music was accompanied by two kindergarten bands. Some of the tots were in buggies, carts, and decorated tricycles and vehicles.

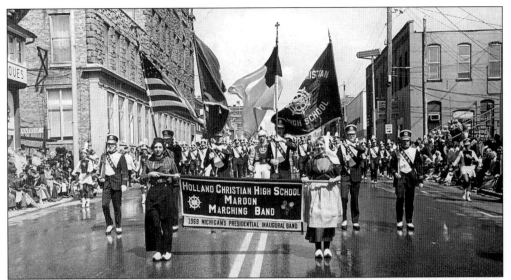

At the 1971 festival, Holland Christian High School's band remembered marching in Washington, D.C. in 1969 as Michigan's Presidential Inaugural Band.

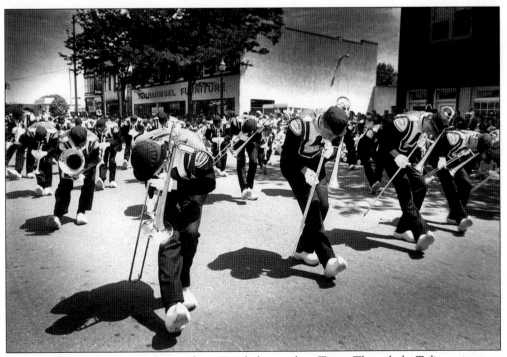

Holland High School's Dutch Marching Band always plays *Tiptoe Through the Tulips* as it struts during the festival parades. The band has been wearing wooden shoes since the 1958 festival.

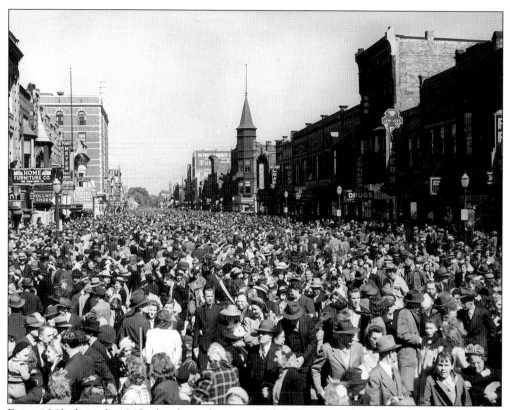

From 1942 through 1945, the festival was curtailed to just a flower show. After the 1946 resumption of a full-fledged Tulip Time, throngs of people filled the street following the Saturday Parade of Bands. The Saturday parade is now called Muziekparade.

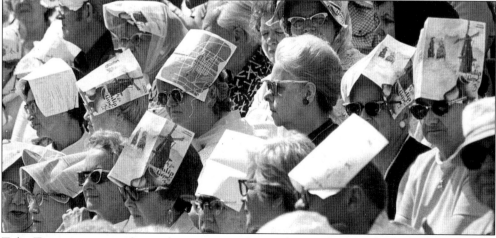

Tulip Time programs make good sun visors, unless you've just been to the hair salon.

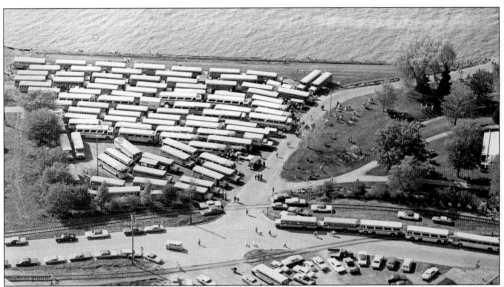

In 1971, visiting busses found a parking place south of Kollen Park.

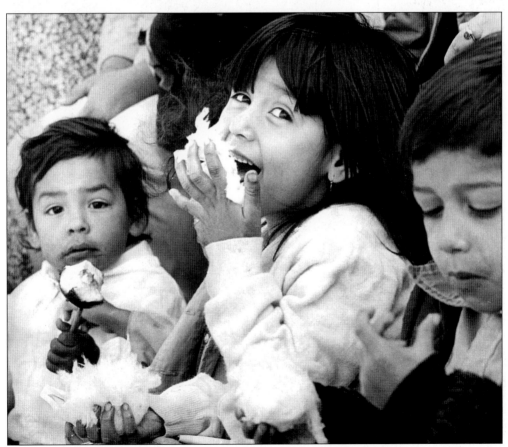

Eating cotton candy and a candy apple are always part of Tulip Time fun.

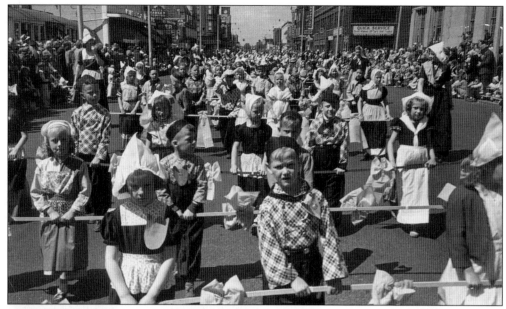

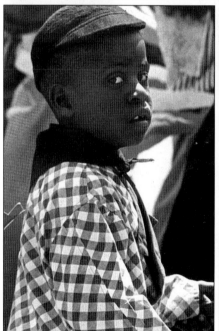

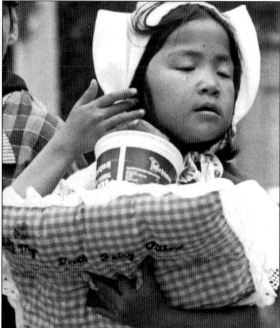

These elementary youngsters kept their lines straight by holding on to long sticks. Most of the children remembered a life in Holland when more than 85 percent of the residents were of Dutch descent. Accompanied by their teachers, these children are walking on River Avenue 50 years ago, when the Children's Parade turned on Eighth Street and continued south on River Avenue to Twelfth Street. Now the event, called Kinderparade, stays on Eighth Street and heads west to Kollen park.

Holland has been the site of a blossoming African-American community for the last 15 years.

The Asian population is represented by more than 4,000 residents in the Holland area, a community that has grown significantly during the last two decades.

In the 1969 Children's Parade, this Dutch-costumed eight-year-old lad, Kenneth Stam, has constructed his paper tulip, complete with stem and bud, surely hoping his mother will observe him and his project.

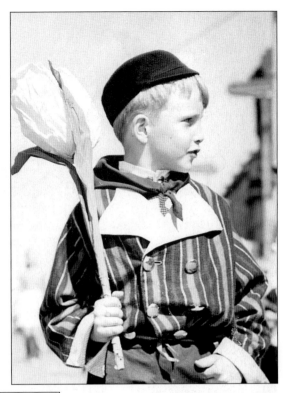

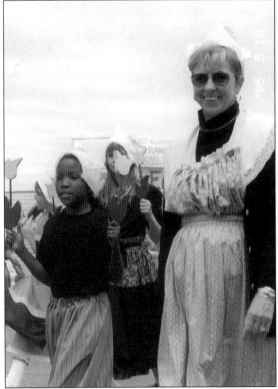

Quinette Yarbrough walks next to her teacher, Mary Vande Water, in the 1995 Children's Parade. In 2000, Miss Yarbrough was crowned queen of the first African-American festival in Holland. Called Juneteenth, the celebration began that year.

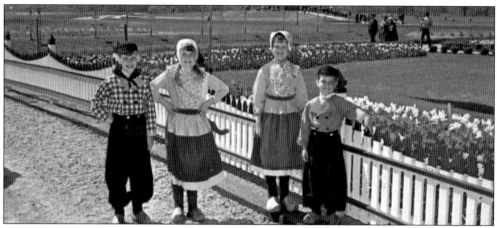

Windmill De Zwaan presents the perfect opportunity for a photo of these elementary school children, a decade after the windmill became a tourist attraction. Nancy Vande Water (second from right) and Barbara Miller are dressed in Isle of Marken costumes while John Miller and William Klomparens are wearing Voldendam costumes. More than a million and a half people have visited the 240-year-old, 125-foot windmill called *De Zwaan*.

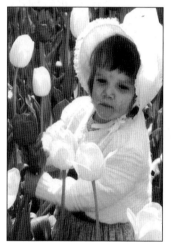

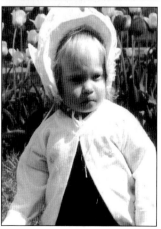

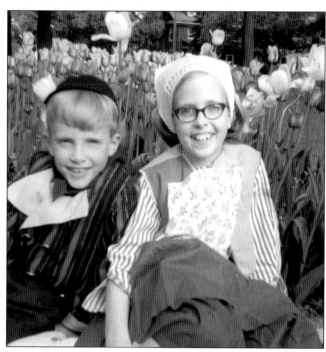

Ken and Kathy Stam pose in a bed of Centennial Park tulips 33 years ago.

People of all ages, including pre-schoolers (left), are dressed for Tulip Time. Pictures of people posing in the tulip beds fill many photo albums in Holland. With bonnets and Dutch hats, two-year-old twins Alexandra and Nicole Stam were pictured among Darwin tulips in 1995.

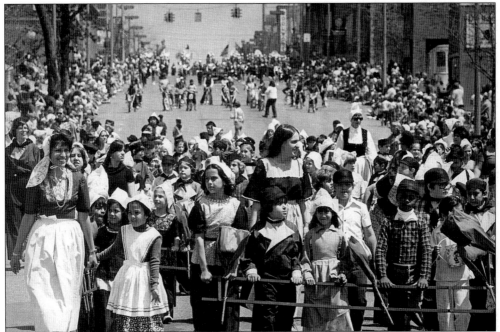

For more than a quarter of a century, the diversity of Holland has changed considerably, and the town's colorful future is evidenced in the Children's (Kinder) Parade. More than 7,000 students from the community's public, private, parochial, charter, and home schools participate. This 1982 group is from Washington Elementary School, and the teachers include Margaret Krause, David Hemmeke, Connie Nieto, Pam Mastos, and aide Jackie Tonno.

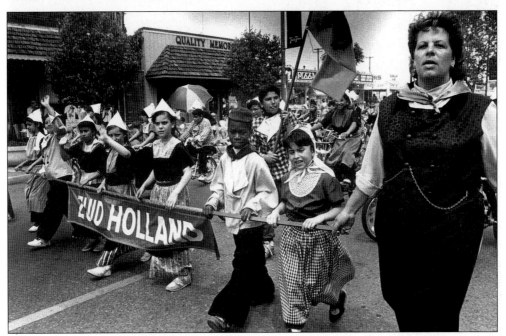

Carrying their banners, plus bicycles and flags, these third grade students in 1991 are from Lincoln Elementary School.

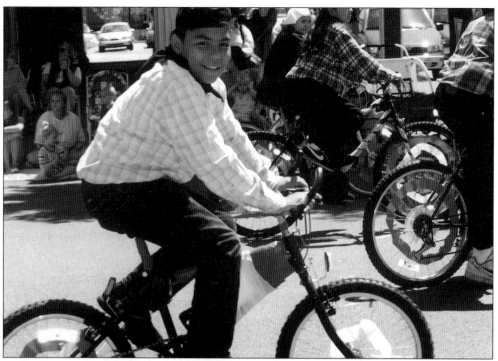

Tony Vasquez rides his decorated bicycle in the Children's (Kinder) Parade.

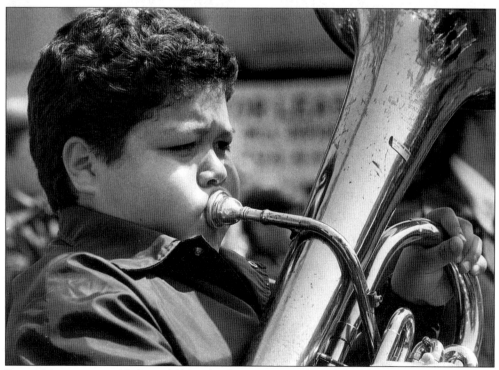

Sergio Mascorro, age 12, heartily blew his horn as a member of the Seventh Grade Band in a 1989 parade.

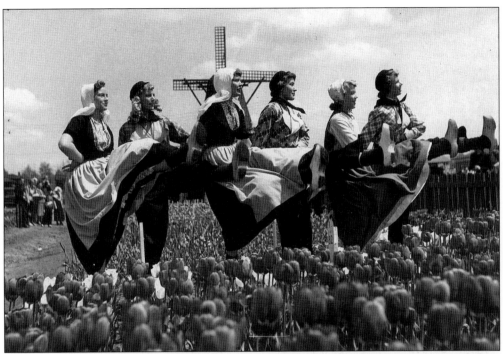
Klompen dancers pose for a magazine photographer among beds of tulips at the tulip farms.

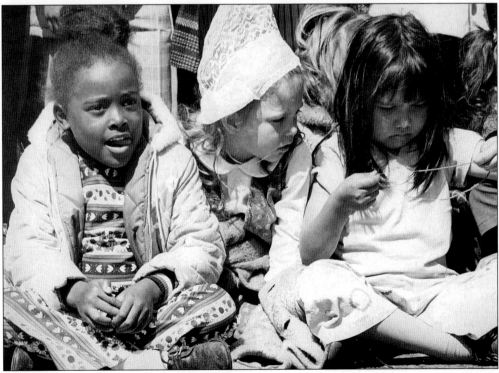
These girls of varied ethnic backgrounds wait for a 1971 parade, indicating Holland's population and diversity was changing.

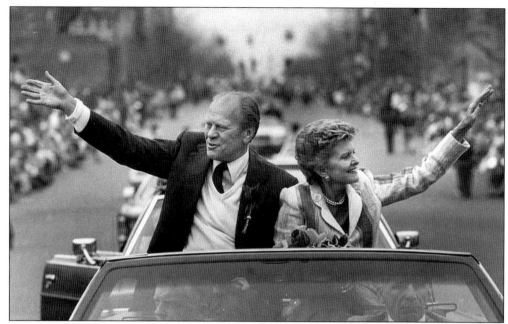

Former President and Mrs. Gerald R. Ford returned to Holland to be grand marshals of the 1978 Parade of Bands. First elected to Congress in 1948, Ford served Holland, a part of the Fifth District, until appointed president in 1974.

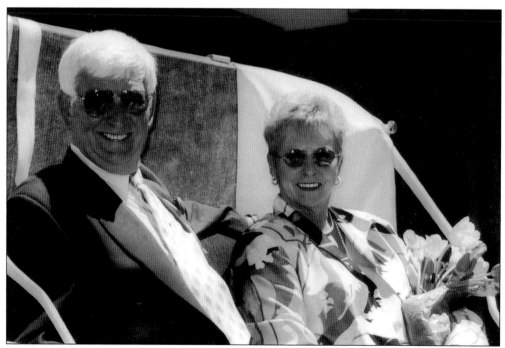

Mr. and Mrs. Randall P. Vande Water rode in a horse-driven carriage in the 2001 tulip festival. Vande Water, formerly Managing Editor of *The Holland Sentinel*, was honored as grand marshal of the Muziekparade (formerly Parade of Bands) for his many years of participation in festival and civic activities in the community.